Tranquility

BY TUESDAY

Other Works by Laura Vanderkam

168 Hours

All the Money in the World

What the Most Successful People Do Before Breakfast

I Know How She Does It

Off the Clock

Juliet's School of Possibilities

The New Corner Office

Tranquility

BY TUESDAY

9 Ways to Calm the Chaos
and Make Time for
What Matters

LAURA VANDERKAM

PORTFOLIO | PENGUIN

Portfolio / Penguin
An imprint of Penguin Random House LLC
penguinrandomhouse.com

Most Portfolio books are available at a discount when purchased in quantity
for sales promotions or corporate use. Special editions, which include
personalized covers, excerpts, and corporate imprints, can be created when
purchased in large quantities. For more information, please call (212) 572-2232
or email specialmarkets@penguinrandomhouse.com. Your local bookstore
can also assist with discounted bulk purchases using the Penguin Random
House corporate Business-to-Business program. For assistance in locating
a participating retailer, email B2B@penguinrandomhouse.com.

ISBN 9780593419007 (hardcover)
ISBN 9780593419014 (ebook)

Printed in the United States of America
1st Printing

BOOK DESIGN BY FINE DESIGN

All participant quotes are from the Tranquility by Tuesday
project survey responses or follow-up interviews.

For Henry

CONTENTS

INTRODUCTION

*W*e all have 24 hours in a day. We all live through the same 168 hours each week. Yet during certain seasons of life, we experience those hours in more intense ways than we do in others.

If you are picking up this book, then perhaps you are living through such a whirlwind time. Mornings are a rush of getting people out the door. Workdays feature their drumbeat of meetings and deadlines. Evenings descend more quickly than seems possible. You wake up on Monday and realize, when you stop to breathe, that it is suddenly Thursday. Weekends require their own sets of marching orders to ensure that everyone arrives where they are supposed to go at approximately the time that they said they would. Hours must give all that you ask of them.

I am living through these busy years too. Any day in my own suburban circus can feature the ridiculousness that comes from raising my five children—Jasper, Sam, Ruth, Alex, and Henry—ranging in age from teens to a toddler. My husband Michael and I manage the logistics of two careers where there is always something else we could be doing. During the recent pandemic years, we elected to raise the degree of difficulty by buying and renovating a historic house and bringing home a puppy. All of this is chosen and, indeed, hoped for. It also results in days when life feels like an act where a clown spins half a dozen plates on poles. Someone has a before-school meeting and a contractor can suddenly come repair a long-broken appliance. The dog needs to be elsewhere while I am giving a virtual speech, and a late-night video conference means the kid who normally uses my laptop for online tutoring needs a different machine.

Perhaps you have also found yourself in a ring in this circus. Perhaps you thrust yourself there or perhaps you simply woke up to realize that the moving parts had multiplied while you weren't paying attention. You can keep the plates spinning. With your calendars and your planners you are very good at that, but the performance can consume so much effort that it is easy to become aggravated about little things. Life can feel like a slog. Years can slip through your fingers, disappearing into a general sense of distress or fatigue over spending too much brainpower worrying about each day's logistics.

I have spent the last decade and a half writing about time management. I have seen thousands of people's schedules. I have talked with them about their struggles. I have come to see that it is a lament against this malaise that people are most often voicing when they ask successful types, "How do you do it?" It is not so much a question of how to organize a summer schedule, or run meetings that start and end on time, important as those skills are. Fundamentally, people want to know how to *enjoy* whatever time they have on this planet. They want to stop feeling like they're either racing against the clock or wishing time away. Maybe we need our minutes to give all that we ask of them, but because the plates are not going to magically stop spinning, and because we don't truly wish for fewer plates, we need to learn to calm the chaos and find joy in busy days. There is no sense in waiting for vacations—hardly relaxing if you've still got your toddler, only now he's off his usual schedule—or some elusive future. Life is not going to be less hectic next week. Life probably won't be less hectic next year. We have to make time for what matters now. We need practical, straight-forward strategies to make that happen.

Lessons from time logs

Tranquility is the state of being serene and peaceful, of being free from agitation. When I first began pondering this word, I imag-ined silent meditation in some mountain retreat. There would be no leaf blowers. There would be no incessant pounding from a neighbor's roof renovation project.

But the more I thought about it, the more I realized that serenity isn't noteworthy if life is serene around you. When recovering alcoholics pray the famous Serenity Prayer, asking for the "serenity to accept the things I cannot change" and "courage to change the things I can," they are not usually facing down a life where all is going great. The goal is tranquility even when life is complicated, challenging, and occasionally chaotic.

A reader once expressed this desire to me as "waking up and looking forward to what's ahead, because I know there is a plan in place no matter what dilemmas occur." I want strategies that make life feel better—more manageable and more joyful—even on a Tuesday when I am driving kids to activities and squeezing in podcast recordings when another neighbor's high-decibel tree-trimming service is taking their breaks.

And so, as I've studied people's schedules, and shared what I've learned in my talks and books, I have tried the most promising strategies in my own life. Over the past decade or so, I have narrowed all these ideas down to nine practical rules with the biggest impact:

1. Give yourself a bedtime
2. Plan on Fridays
3. Move by 3 p.m.
4. Three times a week is a habit
5. Create a back-up slot
6. One big adventure, one little adventure

7. Take one night for you
8. Batch the little things
9. Effortful before effortless

These catchphrases all center around deeper concepts in time management, which this book will explore, but they also suggest straightforward actions. When I follow these nine rules, my life feels better. I feel more in control of the careening pieces. My life feels rich and full—like I am making better use of whatever time I've been given, not doing stuff just to put stuff on the calendar, but because I wish to be a good steward of life's possibilities. I am able to say yes to opportunities when I see them. I make space for the writing, running, singing, reading, and adventures that give me the energy to do everything else I need to do.

I've seen these strategies work for other people who are deep into the busy years of building careers and raising families as well.

For instance, one couple, whose evening time together disappeared once their little kids became older kids who didn't go to bed by 8 p.m., learned my rule that "Three times a week is a habit." They looked at their weekly schedules and found times they could share lunch, grab a drink at a neighborhood bar while their old-enough-to-stay-home-alone kids amused themselves, and chat for a few weekend minutes on the porch, recasting downtime as couple time.

A professor who needed time to write articles for publication—but who would often see this time lost to teaching responsibilities—learned my rule to "Create back-up slots." These slots meant that what mattered happened, even when life didn't go as planned. Unsurprisingly, her submission pace accelerated.

A busy software engineer with three young kids learned my rule to "Take one night for you," apart from work and family responsibilities. It was a nudge to set up a weekly tennis game with her sisters, which massively increased the amount of joy in her life.

The Tranquility by Tuesday project

I love the notes I receive about these transformations. I love hearing about the upgrades people have made in their schedules, and about the positive changes people make in their communities when they are no longer feeling frazzled and overwhelmed. But anecdotes aren't evidence on their own. It is a big world. A determined sleuth can find anecdotes about anything. When I recommend something, I want to know that this self-help is reliably helpful.

To determine that, I needed people to test my rules systematically and report back on what changed in their lives.

So, to figure out whether these rules worked for anyone beyond me and those who'd found my email address, I conducted what I called the Tranquility by Tuesday project in the spring of 2021. This was a time use and perception study. I looked at whether busy people could make practical changes in their lives that would lead to them feeling better about their time. I collected quantitative data on time satisfaction. I collected copious observations from participants about their lives and schedules as well.

Approximately 150 people completed this ten-week program. Most participants (65 percent) worked more than thirty-five hours per week for pay; 71 percent had kids under age eighteen living at home.

At the beginning of the study, people completed a one-day time log, reporting how they spent the previous day. This helped me understand their baseline behaviors and attitudes toward time. They answered how much they disagreed or agreed (on a 7-point scale) with various statements of time satisfaction, such as "Yesterday, I made progress on my professional goals" and "Yesterday, I had enough energy to handle my responsibilities." (Please see my full time-satisfaction scale in the Appendix.) They answered questions about their particular concerns, and about what was working well and what wasn't.

I had some concern that busy people would give cursory responses to my open-ended questions. I shouldn't have worried. When primed to reflect on their hours, and their lives, people shared profoundly personal thoughts about how hard it was to calm the chaos and make time for what matters—thoughts that will feel familiar to anyone hurtling through the busy years.

- "I usually end up doing things last minute and being very stressed out about it."
- "I always feel like I am running to catch up with everything, and very rarely like I have it all under control, despite what I think is a pretty good planning system."
- "I have a bad habit of completely overestimating what I can accomplish in a day or week. I allow myself to make unrealistic to-do lists, and then I feel guilty for not getting enough done."
- "I'm frittering time away with stuff: tidying, managing, upkeep."
- "We are understaffed in my department, but between the short daycare hours, my one-plus hour commute, and general burnout, I feel challenged to get my work done in the week and often have to work during nap times on the weekend."
- "There are too many meetings about nothing."
- "I am thinking about kid stuff while at work, and work stuff while with the kids."
- "My work to-do list is never ending. I have tried multiple ways to prioritize and nothing ever sticks. I have a list of personal to-dos to work on during lunch hour, and then work through lunch. I have a list of personal to-dos to

work on after dinner, but after washing dishes, I just have no energy . . . So I just feel like I'm always putting stuff off."

- "Life feels chaotic with so many different balls in the air and it feels stressful and overwhelming at times."
- "I get all of my daily tasks done, but struggle to make progress on long-term projects or goals."
- "Although we are with the children a lot, I feel like we don't do anything of quality with them at the moment."
- "I have little time to myself so I end up staying up really late to get it."
- "There is too much wasted leisure time doomscrolling rather than doing something I would find relaxing."
- "I love to read, love to exercise, love to cook for fun—but I feel guilty when I do these things, even if the time presents itself. I'm so tuned in to always feeling like I should be doing something productive, ticking something off a list, that I don't get as much joy out of those activities as I once did. **Guilt-free leisure time is very elusive.**"
- "I always feel like I need a few more hours each day in order to have time to manage family and life."

The news wasn't all bleak. As people reflected on their time logs and their lives, they saw many good things. They were getting a lot done. They met their deadlines. Their children got where they needed to go. And yet many people reported that they felt like they spent all their time "either working or taking care of the kids," as one person put it. There was little time for things that would bring more joy and meaning to their days.

I understand all these challenges. I also believe it is possible to take practical steps to address these challenges, even in the busy years when minutes feel scarce. We are never going to get extra hours in the day, so we need to learn to work with what we have.

Nine weeks, nine rules

For nine weeks after filling out the initial survey, participants received a few weekly emails. On Fridays, I sent a short description of a time-management strategy. Participants then answered a few questions about how they planned to use the week's rule in their lives. I asked them to anticipate challenges, and to think about how they might address those challenges. On Mondays, I sent a reminder email about the strategy. On Thursdays, I sent a follow-up email with a survey asking how the week had gone. How had people implemented each rule in their lives? What worked? What didn't? Did they plan to keep using the rule? I also asked whether they were continuing to use the previous weeks' rules.

At the end of nine weeks, participants received a follow-up survey with a one-day time log, and more questions about how they felt about their time. I followed up one month and three months later to see which rules had stuck.

The good news is that these nine practical strategies do make life feel better. People's time-satisfaction scores improved with a high degree of statistical significance between the initial survey and the post-project survey. People's satisfaction with how they spent time "generally" rose 16 percent from the beginning of the project to the end of the nine weeks. Satisfaction with how people spent time "yesterday" rose 17 percent.

As a cohort, my participants improved on every single time measure, but some of the biggest jumps came in how happy people were with their leisure time. They were far less likely to feel like they were frittering time away. Measured agreement with the statement "Yesterday, I was happy with how I spent my leisure time" rose 20 percent from the initial to final survey. Agreement with the statement "Yesterday, I didn't waste time on things that weren't important to me" jumped 32 percent from the beginning to the end.

These numbers made me happy, but people's reflections were the most rewarding to read. In the time log accompanying the final survey, I saw a surprising number of exclamation points as people reflected on the impact these rules had on their lives. They gave more specific details, reflecting better recall of how the day before had been spent (recall scores rose 7 percent from the initial to the final survey). They could see what their time choices had made possible. As one participant noted, "I woke up at 6:30 feeling very rested, because I had gone to bed by my 10/10:30 bedtime the night before," and that "I was very productive during my work hours because I had a clear sense of what I needed to do (thanks to planning my week in advance)."

This sense of time satisfaction even came through on time logs that contained challenging situations. One participant following the "One big adventure, one little adventure" rule had planned a picnic lunch with a friend, and then realized, as she was about to head out, that someone had stolen the catalytic converter from her car.

It appears, from her log, that she got another ride and went to the picnic anyway.

The Tranquility by Tuesday project "has encouraged me to be intentional about building in time for joy and restoration," one participant wrote. Wrote another: "The biggest surprise was how simple each [rule] was to do, yet how much difference it made each week. Maybe not perfect, but even partial implementation made a difference."

I believe that you will experience the same results in your life. Follow these nine rules, and you too will be more satisfied with your time—both generally, and in how you spend your hours on a run-of-the-mill Tuesday.

How you should read this book

Each chapter of this book covers one of these nine ways of calming the chaos and making time for what matters: why it works, the philosophy behind it, and how you might use it in your life, as my project participants did in theirs. Broadly, these rules fit in three categories:

First come the foundational strategies, which boost well-being but also encourage thinking about time more strategically.

Then we look at strategies for making good things happen—learning how to consciously build more enjoyable activities into a schedule, no matter what life dishes up.

Then the last section looks at how to waste less time—that is, how to spend less time doing things that, in the long run, most of us would like to spend less time doing.

To maximize the impact of these rules on your life, I'd recommend reading through the book once to become familiar with the rules. Then you can go back through and begin trying the rules in order. You could layer them on week by week, as people in the Tranquility by Tuesday project did, or even month by month if you wanted to make a longer project out of it. For each rule, ask yourself the planning questions at the end of the chapter; these will help you think about how the rule might work in your life, and if you anticipate challenges, how you might address them. After you've tried the rule for a while, ask yourself the implementation questions. How did the strategy work? Did you need to make changes? Did you face the expected challenges, or different ones? If so, what can you do about those?

A few of the rules ("Effortful before effortless") can be followed immediately. Others ("Plan on Fridays") need a few weeks before the full effects can be seen. A few ("Take one night for you") might require a longer time frame to make happen, particularly if you decide to commit to something big. If you read through the book once, and then go back to create a one-rule-at-a-time schedule, you could take these differences into account.

I would suggest going in order, because the rules build on one another. You may discover, as you read the book, that you are already following some of these rules, at least some of the time. Many of the Tranquility by Tuesday project participants reported being dedicated students of productivity literature, which is why it was exciting to me that their time-satisfaction scores rose as much as they did. We can all use reminders to stick with our good habits. For any advanced-level readers, each chapter also has a bonus strategy that you can try after you've made the primary strategy a habit. As you take the next step, these tweaks can help you see more benefits in your life.

On the other hand, some of the rules might not seem useful to you. People's lives are different. While I consider the Tranquility by Tuesday rules to be broadly applicable, they are going to be most transformative for the categories of people who have less discretionary time, usually because of full-time work and caregiving commitments. You might also think you simply couldn't follow a few of these rules for some reason or another. That might be true. You know your circumstances best. However, sometimes resistance is interesting in its own right. Exactly why do you think that a rule won't work? A strong reaction might be worth exploring. Other busy people have found it possible and helpful to move by 3 p.m., or to leave some open space in their lives, and so forth. Sometimes a strong reaction means that a strategy is challenging assumptions that haven't been challenged in a while. You might sit with this discomfort and see what comes of it.

As for those folks who don't like rules? "If calling them rules will make them seem too rigid, think of them as guidelines and don't worry if they don't all work great for you," one participant suggested. "Adding a few good guidelines is much better than none at all." You could call these rules "experiments" and consider trying them out to be the iterative process of life design. You aren't committing to anything. You can play with a concept for a week and move on. It might not help at all. Or you might be surprised. You don't know until you try.

You can work through the Tranquility by Tuesday rules on your own. But if you feel more accountable when others are involved, then read this book with a friend or two. Read a chapter, send your planning answers to one another, and then check back for your implementation answers a week later. Together, you can keep one another on track.

Happiness happens in hours

Achieving tranquility amid the frenzy of modern life is challenging. It is certainly more challenging than basic time-management matters, such as figuring out how long it will take to pack for a trip. It is also a more nebulous goal than landing a promotion or a big new client. But my guess is that you are already a productive and ambitious person.

So I'm going to promise something different. I want you to feel better about your time. If you use these nine strategies in your life, I believe that you will feel more satisfied with your hours. You will be happier with your leisure time, and you will be more mindful of its existence. You will even be better able to describe how you spend your time, because more of your time will be spent intentionally on what brings you joy. And you will become quite serious about that joy—so dedicated to it that you will figure out a way to get to your picnic when a theft renders Option A inadvisable. Other people, just like you, felt 17 percent more satisfied with how they spent yesterday after learning these rules. They felt like they wasted less time, even in lives that didn't suggest a lot of wasted time in the first place.

I want the same for you.

When we think about "joy" and "happiness," we often think about whether the big pieces of a good life are in place: the prestigious job, the loving family, the beautiful home. These things matter, but happiness is actually experienced in how we spend our hours. If every day looks the same, if you feel lethargic from sitting too long or exhausted from sleep deprivation, if you rarely have time for the absorbing work you find meaningful, and if you rarely have time for hobbies or to connect with the friends who make you laugh, that prestigious job and loving family can start to feel like a grind. We can berate ourselves for feeling this way.

We try gratitude practices or even post photos on social media with the hashtag #blessed, but resentment can linger.

I want to help you with this predicament. I believe the big pieces of your life are probably good. I don't want to change those. I want to change how you spend an average Tuesday. I want you to know that even an average day will feature levity and purpose. I want you to know good things are coming up, and that when the inevitable crises arise, you will be able to stay on track with your goals, no matter what.

Life is full of possibilities, even in the middle of commutes or Zoom calls. On a recent day when I had to make a second trip to a notary public after making a clerical error on the first form, I did also manage to enjoy a short hike in a new spot (thus making sure to "Move by 3 p.m." and experience the latter half of the "One big adventure, one little adventure" rule). I worked on a thousand-piece puzzle between my baby's bedtime and the big kids' bedtime (in other words, doing "effortful" fun before the effortless variety). And I lovingly but firmly put myself to bed at a reasonable hour ("Give yourself a bedtime"), which made another early toddler morning feel slightly less bleary. I could sit for a few minutes while he played with his toys, sip my coffee, and feel serene.

That lasted for about four minutes before the circus resumed its next kid-screaming, dog-barking act. But, noticed, four minutes can be quite profound.

PART 1

Calm the Chaos

Foundational habits for taking control of your time

*P*icture yourself on a normal Tuesday. Work and family demands are as incessant as always. Yet you feel excited as you wake up. You are well rested. You have the energy to do what you need to do, and when your energy levels inevitably dip through the day, you have a plan to recharge. You survey the day's schedule and see that while it is full, there will be hours devoted to those important-but-not-urgent matters that add joy to your life. You know what needs to happen, and you have a plan to get those things done.

Wouldn't that feel nice?

That is the promise of the first three Tranquility by Tuesday rules. These rules are, on their surface, about general well-being. We want to approach our full lives with energy and optimism. We boost capacity and mood by getting enough sleep and physical activity. Having a general sense of what we need and want to do with our time, and a plan to make these things come to fruition, keeps us from feeling overwhelmed. And so we need to give ourselves a bedtime, plan on Fridays, and move each day by 3 p.m. These foundational habits will, almost immediately, make each day's hours feel better.

But all these rules have a deeper purpose as well. They nudge us to think about time strategically. When we give ourselves a bedtime, we give shape to the day. We start to make more active, mindful choices about what a given day can and cannot contain. When we plan on Fridays, we start to think about our future selves, and how we can make steady progress toward our long-term goals. When we commit to move by 3 p.m., we start to look at even busy days critically, seeing where the space might be, and knowing that we have the power to increase our capacity to do difficult things.

In other words, we become the master craftsmen of our schedules. First, we survey our days, then we shape our weeks, then we narrow in on our hours. As we become more familiar with the material, we grow more skillful. The foundation is laid to make something beautiful. And that makes us excited, on any given Tuesday, to get out of bed.

RULE 1

Give Yourself a Bedtime

Going to bed earlier is how grown-ups sleep in.

Somewhere, on the blurry edge of memory, I picture a scene. I am in my little brother's childhood room. He and I are creating elaborate plot lines for our Playmobil figures. By day, they run a school, a hotel, a tap dancing ensemble. Then fictional evening descends. We put the children to bed. The adults? We announce, with knowing smiles, that they are going to *stay up all night*.

I laugh at this now, this idea that staying up all night would be a privilege of adulthood. Come actual adulthood, I feel like I spend much of my energy some days convincing the younger people in my house to go to bed so I can go to bed. There is always something else that has to happen. The toddler wants to be rocked again. Someone else's homework must go in the back-pack. Someone has forgotten to tell me something very import-ant, some story that takes meandering minutes to come to its conclusion.

I love sleep. I'd like to think sleep loves me back. But sleep and I have had to work hard to maintain our relationship during these years with babies and—my own particular middle-aged dilemma—early-rising little kids and night-owl teenagers. I have become an acute observer of sleep's quirks. Some fantastical dream suddenly introduces the plot twist of a crying child—and then, in a few minutes, the dream itself has disappeared and I am in my room with an actual sleepless kid. During the infant phases when I was waking and falling back asleep multiple times per day, I learned to recognize when, exactly, sleep was starting to visit. My mind would drift somewhere related to my life and then, as a familiar weight settled, I would see some scene that could not really be happening. I dreamed lucidly at times, partic-ularly during the naps my poorly sleeping babies necessitated. I was aware, but thinking things I normally would not.

I know the bleary resignation of facing down a day without enough sleep. I know the particular despair of doing it multiple nights in a row. And yet I have seen a curious paradox with this—one that affects a great many people during the busy years of raising a family and building a career, and that has important ramifications for how we can best manage our schedules.

I track my time on weekly spreadsheets. All of my time. Since April of 2015, I have recorded how I have spent every half hour of my life. There's no reason for anyone who doesn't study time professionally to do more than a few weeks of this, but the upside of my long-running data gathering is that I know exactly how much I sleep and when I sleep. My data set contains thousands of days. These recorded years include the babyhoods of my two youngest children, including all those middle-of-the-night wake-ups and miserably early weekend mornings.

There have been rough stretches. Yet, one way or another, I hit my sleep set point: 7.3–7.4 hours/day averaged over any given eight weeks or so. That's squarely in the range (seven to nine hours a day) that sleep literature suggests most adults need.

The most rigorous time-diary studies have found that most people do get enough sleep from a quantitative perspective. The American Time Use Survey, which has thousands of people talk through how they spent the previous 4 a.m. to 4 a.m. day, usually covering all 365 days of the year, found that in 2020, the average person slept 9.01 hours in a twenty-four-hour period (up from 8.84 hours in 2019). In 2019, employed parents with kids under age six averaged 8.32 hours (8.26 for men; 8.39 for women). No one ever believes me when I mention this statistic, but my own time-diary studies of people with jobs and kids, which have had people record how they spent the previous day, hour by hour, have found averages that are fairly close to eight hours too. For instance, when I had women who held intense professional jobs, and who had children at home, track their time for a week for my book *I Know How She Does It*, I found that they averaged 7.7 hours of sleep per day.

This raises the obvious question: Why, exactly, do we feel so tired?

Because there is no doubt that many of us do. It is an important question, because sleep is foundational for all other good habits. Fatigue makes it harder to think strategically about the future, or to make good choices with time. Being adequately rested boosts performance on cognitively difficult tasks. We are less distracted. It is simply easier to be productive when you've gotten enough sleep.

I've studied thousands of time logs over the years in an attempt to reconcile how people can, when their time is tracked, seem to be sleeping enough, and yet still claim, in many polls, to sleep low amounts on a "typical" night, or to talk of sleep, as sociologist Arlie Hochschild once wrote, "the way a hungry person talks about food."

I have come away convinced that the culprit is *disorderly sleep*. A reasonable average hides that people are often undershooting and then overshooting in a way that leads to fatigue on some days and an inability to maintain good routines on the others. This reality is obvious enough for people with babies, or those who do shift work, but is surprisingly widespread. For instance, in one of my time-diary studies, I found that 22 percent of people slept at least 90 minutes more, or less, on Tuesday than they did on Wednesday. That is a big gap.

Asked about a typical night, someone might report sleeping from midnight to 6 a.m. A time log shows that this did, indeed, happen twice in the past week. But two other nights, this person crashed on the couch in front of the TV at 10 p.m., or fell asleep for an hour while putting a child to bed, or hit snooze three times on Thursday, with weekends looking completely different. The mental picture is six hours. The average might be 7.5, but each day is undershooting or overshooting in a way that wreaks havoc on someone's ability to function. If people are always undershooting or overshooting, that would explain why the National Sleep Foundation's annual Sleep in America poll found that, in 2020, people reported feeling sleepy, on average, three days per week. Overshot days don't feel particularly great either, when people sleep through their alarms, or however else their bodies force them to substitute sleep for other activities. Far better to hit the ideal each day.

We can't always control when we sleep. But given how important sleep is for flourishing, when it is possible to steer clear of that drop-tower carnival ride of skimping and then catching up, life can feel more calm. Since most adults need to wake at set times for work or family responsibilities, the only variable that can move is the time we go to sleep the night before.

In other words, despite what I fantasized about with my Playmobil characters, even adults need a bedtime. They need to go to bed on time, at a set time. And so that is **Tranquility by Tuesday Rule 1: Give yourself a bedtime**.

If you would like to experience the additional energy and optimism that comes from being well rested, choose a time that you would like to go to sleep more nights than not. Then, commit

to getting in bed by that time unless you have a compelling reason not to.

How to put yourself to bed

Figuring out and implementing a bedtime is a simple, four-step
process.

1. Decide when you plan to wake up most weekdays.

Be honest. While it might be fun to fantasize about waking
up at 4 a.m. to run ten miles and meditate for thirty minutes before making yourself a kale smoothie, if you have not
done any of those things in the past week, you are not going
to start now. What wake-up time makes the most sense for
your life as it actually is? If you tend to be woken by your
young children, track your time for a few weeks to establish
a bell curve of when they are up for good. You can set a waking time at the point where most of the wake-ups occur after
that.

2. Decide how much sleep you need.

Let's be honest here too. Most working-age adults need between seven and nine hours per day, with the majority of

those landing between seven and eight. Few people need less than six and a half hours per day, aside from a handful of genetic short sleepers who sleep short hours on weekends and vacations too. If you aren't sure, aim for seven and a half hours and see how it goes. If you're still crashing on weekends, you need more. If you wake up consistently before your alarm clock, you might need less.

3. Calculate what time you need to be in bed in order to get this amount of sleep.

This is a math problem. If you need to wake up at 6 a.m. on most weekday mornings, and you need seven and a half hours of sleep, then count back seven and a half hours. This gives you a 10:30 p.m. bedtime. If you need to wake up at 8 a.m., then you can go to bed at 12:30 a.m. Giving yourself a bedtime doesn't mean you have to go to bed at the same time you did when you were ten years old. If you are a night owl who doesn't have to be up before 10 a.m., feel free to choose a bedtime that reflects that.

The important thing is to be consistent. If your life allows leeway on weekends, then you can shift by an hour or so, but any more will make Monday morning more painful than necessary. And if you've got young children who don't understand the concept of weekends, then you're best off sticking with the same bedtime nightly, and building your evenings with this bedtime in mind.

4. Set an alarm for fifteen to thirty minutes before the official bedtime so you can ease into bed.

This last step is key. If you don't start winding down until your actual bedtime, you will go to bed later than you intend to. So start the process at least fifteen minutes before. If you want to read for more than a few minutes, or have some couple time, set your bedtime alarm earlier. Turn off the lights when the moment arrives. Try this for a week and see how it goes. Since most adults can't really "sleep in," at least during the week, then going to bed on time is the best way to recreate this sense of on-vacation-with-no-kids luxury.

Participant perspectives: Identifying obstacles

After introducing the "Give yourself a bedtime" rule, I asked the Tranquility by Tuesday project participants to go through the four-step process of figuring out their own bedtimes.

They set desired wake-up times between an eye-opening 3:30 a.m. and 8:30 a.m. They reported needing between six to nine hours of sleep, with a mean of 7.71 hours. They needed, on average, thirty minutes to wind down. For someone with a desired wake-up time of 6 a.m., needing 7.75 hours of sleep, this suggests a 10:15 p.m. bedtime, with the bedtime alarm going off around 9:45 p.m. to allow for thirty minutes of winding down.

For someone with a desired wake-up time of 7 a.m., needing seven hours of sleep and an hour before that to read and relax, this suggests a midnight bedtime, with the bedtime alarm going off around 11 p.m.

People were relatively open-minded about trying this rule, even if they had struggled with consistent sleep in the past. Just a handful of respondents flagged this rule as not being right for them. That said, those who were game to try it could identify numerous challenges to implementing this seemingly simple practice.

Some, like me, had babies or toddlers. A little voice yelling "Dada!" or "Mama!" from a crib at 10:30 p.m. will definitely derail a 10:30 p.m. bedtime.

A number of people mentioned work as a challenge. Sometimes this was a side gig, such as translating papers after the kids went to bed, or answering questions from Etsy customers long into the night. More often, though, it was a quick email check at 10 p.m. that turned into an hour-long back-and-forth conversation.

Some people with older children mentioned the difficulty of getting them into bed on time, which then delayed parental bedtimes.

Some people scurried around getting the household ready for the next day—packing lunches and bags and setting out outfits or cleaning the kitchen. This practice is common, but it's also a Catch-22, because staying up too late to make the next morning go smoothly almost guarantees that the next morning will be dreadful.

A number of people mentioned the difficulty of mustering the energy to begin the bedtime process; one person wrote of being "too tired to get ready (stupid as that sounds)." But silly as it seems, the struggle is real; some research has suggested that we become less disciplined as the day goes on. Turning off the TV and going upstairs to brush teeth takes energy at a time when most people are depleted. It is easier to push the decision later, and then crash on the couch.

Some people's partners observed different hours, which meant that a personally realistic bedtime would shift a family's rhythms. This is never easy to do.

The most poignant problem, though, had nothing to do with work, or housework, or family members; rather, it had to do with their absence. People noted that going to bed means deciding that the day is over. You are making that decision when the house is quiet, the chores are done, and you can finally spend your time as you wish. As one respondent put it, "That's the only truly free time I have." Who wants to cut that short?

This realization came up again and again. One respondent put off sleep because she was "feeling like I didn't have enough leisure time yet." Another reported that "Dad gets distracted with video games or other projects." Couple time and screen time often merged together. "My partner and I usually watch one episode of a TV show on the couch while eating dinner at the end of the day . . . and then just kind of stay on the couch," one person wrote. It wasn't exactly a gourmet meal by candlelight, but for an average Tuesday, it felt pleasant enough.

During the busy years of building a career and raising a family, late-night hours are prime "me time." Indeed, this span of a few hours is often the longest stretch of leisure time that people get. We don't want to end this pleasant, autonomous time by going to sleep. This is doubly true if we haven't seen our partners much during the day and want some time with them. Sometimes the inner rebel emerges—the one who resents childhood's rules dictating lights-out time, and whose Playmobil figures subsequently kept doing their thing into the wee hours. *You can't make me*, the voice goes. *I don't want to go to bed.*

Since no one can stretch a day past its twenty-four-hour limit, sleep can seem like a zero-sum game. As one respondent described this realization, "Spending more time asleep means spending less time doing anything else. So I had to accept that some other things would not get done. Or, spend time doing them but accept I would get less sleep."

If those other things feel compelling enough, we might decide, as Jerry Seinfeld once joked, that a lack of sleep is "Morning Guy's problem."

How to minimize the resentment

I have certainly willed the minutes to move slower once the kids are in bed. It is so tempting to stretch this space out. And yet I know that with early wake-ups pending, a late night will mean a far-less-tranquil morning. Even in the years of life when I haven't had a toddler, going to bed on time means I can wake well rested and able to run (something I won't do at 10 p.m.) or write when I am able to think straight (again, harder to do as the night goes on). Late-night "me time" feels good, but play your cards right and morning "me time" can open up more choices. One respondent who confessed to desiring alone time after the kids went to bed figured out that "If I just go to bed earlier I can wake up early (before kids) and get my quiet alone time, and I usually do something higher quality in the morning like read a professional development book over coffee rather than rewatch three episodes of *Friends* at night!"

This expansion of options means that giving yourself a bedtime is less of a zero-sum game than it first appears. I'd also argue that if you cut sleep short by an hour, but then spend two hours on a task instead of one because you are tired and distracted and prone to making mistakes, then you haven't come out ahead. And if you, like many people who are not chronic insomniacs, have a very strong sleep set point—that is, a quantity of sleep your body will force you to average over a few weeks—then **skimping on sleep one night doesn't buy you more time. It just means you crash and make it up somewhere else**. This may not have desirable effects. In the long run, you might be happier watching fewer hours of late-night Netflix if it means you don't sleep through that group bike ride on Saturday mornings.

It is possible to minimize bedtime resentment in a few ways:

1. Make space for leisure at other points in your schedule.

Many of the other Tranquility by Tuesday rules are designed to do just that. Late-night puttering feels less critical when you know you'll be playing in your softball league on Tuesday nights, when you plan on trying a new lunch spot with a work friend on Friday, and when you're regularly finding forty-five extra minutes to read during the day.

2. Remember that you are still in charge.

A bedtime isn't legally binding. It simply nudges a conscious decision. My bedtime is 11 p.m. It probably should be 10:30 p.m., but 11 p.m. feels more reasonable given that I also have teenage children whose phones must be confiscated. Since 11 p.m. is my bedtime, I have come to view 10:30 p.m. as my moment of truth. I evaluate what I am doing to see if I will be getting in bed by 11 p.m. I don't have to. I am an adult! I can, in fact, stay up all night if I want to! If I'm reading a good book, or having a really good conversation with my husband, I can go to bed later.

You can decide not to observe your bedtime on any given night. Maybe you consciously choose to work late one night so you can bill extra time and thus buy yourself a reasonable life the rest of the week. Maybe you choose to get up early two mornings a week to exercise, and on the others, you sleep until the last possible minute. You can adjust as you want.

But in any case, once the clock strikes 10:30 p.m., if I don't have a good reason to stay up late, then I might as well drift toward bed, knowing that Morning Guy will be far happier with me.

Participant perspectives: Creatively overcoming challenges

Tranquility by Tuesday participants had wise ideas for coping with their bedtime challenges.

A few people who chafed at strict rules modified this strategy by giving themselves a bedtime *window*. Rather than give themselves an official bedtime, they decided that this rule meant they would turn out the lights sometime between, say, 10:30 p.m. and 11:15 p.m. This worked particularly well for people who also had a window during which they could wake up in the morning. They might have planned to get up at 6 a.m. to work out, but if lights out was 11:15 p.m. instead of 10:30 p.m., they'd move the alarm to 6:45 a.m. and do something shorter, or choose a different time for exercise. A real rebel might give himself a fake bedtime—say, 10 p.m.—and enjoy blowing through it every single night, knowing that the real bedtime (e.g., 11 p.m.) was still on track to happen. In life, it's good to know yourself.

One person who found mustering the energy to get ready for bed difficult decided to move these getting-ready tasks into earlier, less-fraught spots of the evening: face-washing after dinner, pajamas when the kids were putting on theirs. It can be easier to observe a bedtime if all that's left to do is climb under the covers.

To be sure, this rule did not work for everyone. Shutting down work was hard for people who felt perpetually behind, which was a common woe for families coping with the hybrid and virtual pandemic school schedules that lingered into the months when I conducted my study. One respondent had the seemingly smart idea of sweeping for work issues each night at 9 p.m., which would give her time to resolve them before bedtime. Unfortunately, "This was taken as an indication that I was available to work then, rather than a proactive means to get ahead on problems," she reported, and so she ended up with even more unscheduled late-night work.

The results

Despite these challenges, those who were able to adhere to a bedtime did report sleeping better. On my time-satisfaction scale, a quarter more people agreed that they were getting enough sleep from the beginning of the program to the end. Scores rose 13 percent on the question of whether people had enough energy to handle their responsibilities (though other rules contributed to that increase as well).

In general, people planned to stick with this rule. In my follow-up interviews with respondents, people often mentioned some other rule as making a big splash in their lives, but that this one most changed their day-to-day experience. As one person put it, of all the rules, "Giving myself a bedtime was probably the least sexy but the most useful."

In the reflection questions about this rule, people noted benefits beyond the obvious upsides of not having to drink four cups of coffee to stay awake in meetings (and then sleeping through their alarms the next morning).

"I thought [a bedtime] would make me feel more rested, and it has, but the real bonus is that it's made me choose my evening time more mindfully," one person said. "I know I have to go to bed at 11:30 p.m., so I was aware I was choosing what to do in the four hours after my toddler has gone to bed."

Four hours is *a lot*. Even two hours—a more common experience for people with young kids—can feel luxurious.

To experience this luxury, though, you have to know how much time there is, and when these hours are. Figuring out a bedtime gives shape to this not-insignificant chunk of a schedule.

Indeed, it gives shape to the entire day, which is the bigger concept behind this rule.

Most of us understand that the day has a beginning. We are a bit fuzzier on the notion that *each day has an end*. And yes, the new parents and shift workers of the world don't sleep continuously overnight, but in general, each day has a given chunk of waking hours.

By defining this amount, we start to think of each day as containing a given quantity of temporal space. That time will be filled by something. I maintain that what we fill each day with is largely up to us, based on current choices and those made in the past. Days can contain a lot. I know I enjoy the puzzle—a form of *Tetris*, if you will—of figuring out how to move the pieces around to make much fit within the 16.6 waking hours I experience daily. Defining the day lets us see that the game board is large. It is also not infinite.

Holding these two competing thoughts in mind, people could make smarter decisions about their time.

Choosing a bedtime "made my evenings more purposeful," one person wrote. "Instead of doing activities (cleaning, reading, relaxing, etc.) and then going to bed when I was 'done,' I had a set amount of time until bedtime and had to figure out what I wanted to do during that time."

People reported enjoying their evenings more once they understood their shape. "It feels pleasantly cozy to have enough time to take care of my skin and floss my teeth, instead of just shoveling myself into bed," one participant who decided to start her bedtime routine earlier reported. "It feels nice to have time allotted to read in bed, instead of regarding it as a guilty pleasure."

This enjoyment extended even to couple time, which people worried that a bedtime would curtail. Instead of staying up late working on a project, one person did the math and realized there wasn't going to be enough time before bedtime. So instead this person "got into bed early and spent some extra time winding down and relaxing with my spouse."

Not all couples can set common bedtimes, but for those who can, doing so can increase the chances of spending romantic time together, rather than both of you wiling away hours on the couch until you're too tired to do anything else.

Practicing discipline

Going to bed on time is simple. But it is life-changing—both for the mindset shift it represents about the shape of a day, and for the more obvious reason that being well rested makes even tough days feel doable. We have the willpower to choose joy, rather than simply struggling through the hours.

Choosing to be well rested when it is within our power to be so is about taking "Morning Guy"—or as I like to put it, "Future You"—into account. When facing a decision, you picture yourself on the other side of that decision. You then make a decision to be kind to Future You. You make this decision even if it takes a little effort in the moment. This is the essence of discipline. We think beyond our current impulses to consider the broader ramifications. Going to bed on time is a daily opportunity to practice this discipline. Other Tranquility by Tuesday rules provide the opportunity to strengthen and stretch this muscle in new ways, with what I hope are good results, but this first rule builds the foundation.

And the payoff? For this rule, it is immediate. As people noted:

- "On the evening I went to bed on time and actually slept all night and woke up early enough to exercise and shower before starting my day, I had the best day of the week."
- "Getting enough sleep helped me be my best self both at work and afterward. I have had enough energy to get to everything I have planned this week, and that makes me happy."

Take the next step

CREATE A (BITE-SIZED) MORNING ROUTINE

One of the best reasons to set a bedtime is that it gives you more control over your mornings. Mornings are a great time for getting stuff done. For busy people with careers or young families or both, weekdays tend to feature two potential chunks of autonomous time: at night after the kids go to bed, and first thing in the morning, if you get up early enough. Both have their pleasures, but because many people find it challenging to exercise or do mentally demanding creative work at night, if your aspirations include these activities, mornings might be a better bet.

Mornings also tend to be more regimented than other times of day. Many people wake up and get ready at roughly the same time each day, even if they haven't yet learned the wisdom of giving themselves a bedtime. This means that any good habit built into the regular run-of-show has a high chance of happening.

Plus, there's something very satisfying about achieving a big win before breakfast. Whatever the rest of the day brings, you know you've already done that.

So I am a big fan of morning routines. But don't worry. I'm not asking anyone to commit to a two-hour routine involving a personal trainer and green juice. Indeed, "keeping your routine short and easy to accomplish, especially in the beginning, will greatly increase the chances of you sticking with it," says Benjamin Spall, who ran the popular newsletter *My Morning Routine* for many years. You can always increase the length of the routine over time, but usually, fifteen to thirty minutes is all you need, according to Spall.

So let's start with fifteen minutes. What would you like to do during your mornings, just about every day? Perhaps you are already exercising a few mornings a week, which is wonderful. What other small actions could you add to those mornings, and also do on other mornings, that would have a big payoff over time? I maintain that the focus should be pleasure. What would make you excited to get out of bed, or at least excited to sit down at your desk?

Make a list of two to three bite-sized morning activities that you would genuinely enjoy, and that would positively impact your career, your relationships, or yourself. For instance, you could:

◆ Respond to a creative writing prompt
◆ Read a few pages in a sacred text
◆ Have a cup of coffee outside, weather permitting (or in front of a window if not)

- Take a photo of something beautiful
- Do twenty push-ups and twenty sit-ups
- Do a ten-minute strength-training video
- Meditate with a five-minute program on an app
- Pray a memorized set of prayers
- Pray for a specific person (a new person each day)
- Send an email reaching out to a new or old connection
- Write 250 words in your memoir
- Practice for ten minutes with a foreign-language app
- Read a story in a physical newspaper (or a daily news digest)
- Read one article in a professional journal
- Listen to a short podcast or ten minutes of an audiobook
- Listen to a new piece of music
- Record a quick video for social media
- Stretch or do some yoga poses
- Take several deep breaths and pay attention to your breathing
- Read a story with a young child
- Read a chapter in a book with an older child
- Take care of a few plants
- Have a cup of tea with your spouse
- Check in with a friend, relative, or accountability partner
- Walk to a nearby coffee shop and back home
- Look at your calendar and reflect on the day's priorities

- Write down an intention for the day
- Write a note of praise to an employee or colleague
- Eat a real breakfast

I'm sure you could add many more ideas to this list. In my case, I aim to do three things. I write at least a hundred words in my "free writing file," I do some strength training, and I read a little bit of something big. During 2021, for instance, I read a chapter of *War and Peace* each day. Tolstoy's chapters in his famous epic turn out to be only four to five pages long . . . he just wrote 361 of them. During 2022, I read a few pages of Shakespeare daily, with the goal of making it through his collected works in a year.

In fifteen minutes, you could probably tackle a few bite-sized items. If you like, you could rotate through five or six, choosing three to do each day. Feel free to experiment. There is no right way to do a morning routine. **A morning routine exists to serve you**.

I'd also add that during the busy years, especially with really young children, it might help to view your morning routine as more of a morning "checklist" than as something that has to happen at an exact time. A routine that must happen from 6 a.m. to 6:20 a.m. daily can get derailed by a baby who chooses to wake some morning at 5:55 a.m., or by an early work meeting that requires leaving the house at 6:30 a.m. one morning instead of 7 a.m. By being flexible about the time, you increase the chances of success. Many mornings I do my rituals right after our nanny starts work at 8 a.m. But if I'm needed for the last round of kid shuttling, I'll do them later. On weekends, it might happen well into the afternoon (sometimes "morning" can just be a state of mind). If I'm up before the baby, I might read a chapter on my phone in bed and send myself an email with my free-writing efforts. The kettlebell swings just happen at some other point,

And yes, life can change a routine. Benjamin Spall's morning routine had involved a short meditation, followed by push-ups and sit-ups, followed by working on a writing project. Then, a week or so before I interviewed him, he adopted a six-month-old puppy, and overnight that routine turned into puppy care, including an hour-long walk to drain her energy.

So it goes. People move. People start different jobs. People try working from home. People have new babies. Those babies grow up and start schools that send their buses at comically early hours. In general, when I read about someone's morning routine, I suspect it is a snapshot in time, more than an immovable ideal. But even as the morning routine may change, the concept can still be helpful. Small steps add up over time. Day by day I get a little stronger. I absorb someone else's words that still ring true to the human condition after hundreds of years. I write a little myself and try things out—just for me, just figuring what works, without the pressure to share any of it.

And beyond that? Well, there's always coffee, in my favorite mug, and the light through my office window. There's something about the way it looks in the tranquil early hours that makes me feel that today, like every morning, will be another chance to get it right. And if I went to bed at my bedtime the night before? That makes the morning even better. It's worth giving it a shot.

Your turn

---◆---

GIVE YOURSELF A BEDTIME

Planning questions:

1. What time would you like to wake up most mornings?

2. About how many hours of sleep do you need on an average night?

3. What time do you generally need to be in bed in order to get this amount of sleep? This is your bedtime.

4. About how much time, in minutes, do you need before your bedtime to relax and get ready for bed?

5. Count back from your bedtime, and set an alarm, or some other recurring nudge for this time. What is this time?

6. What might keep you from going to bed at your bedtime?

7. How do you plan to address these challenges?

Implementation questions
(after trying Rule 1 for a week):

1. How did observing a bedtime affect you this week?

2. What challenges did you face in implementing this week's strategy?

3. How did you deal with these challenges?

4. If you were not able to observe a bedtime, what prevented you from doing so?

5. If you needed to modify the rule, how did you do so?

6. How likely are you to continue using this rule in your life?

RULE 2

Plan on Fridays

Expectations are infinite. Time is finite.
We are always choosing. Choose well.

*I*saac Watts, the great hymn writer is best known for lyrics to such songs as "Joy to the World." But I suppose it speaks to my time obsession that I've long been intrigued by a more obscure line in Watts's tribute to Psalm 90. The congregation, usually mumbling by several verses into "O God, Our Help in Ages Past," sings that "Time, like an ever-rolling stream, bears all its sons away."

If you have ever canoed, or gone white-water rafting, you can see the aptness of this metaphor. Moving water moves you along with it. You keep moving whether you think about it or not.

Days, and likewise years, slip into the past. They do this no matter what you do. I see this every Monday morning as I finish filling out my previous week's time log, archive it, and then open a new spreadsheet. The spreadsheet is blank. The upcoming 168 hours are blank. But I know that in 168 hours, that time will have been filled with something. I will be archiving it, same as I have done with the week before, and same as I have done with hundreds of weeks that are now water under the bridge. The stream rolls on.

To keep with the metaphor, during some phases of life, the water seems more swift and turbulent. Floating along on that ever-rolling stream, it is tough to make more than minor course corrections. Perhaps you know this on-edge feeling. You react to whatever rock or eddy springs up. They seem to spring up everywhere. A long-simmering work crisis boils over just as your afterschool sitter quits, the sink springs a leak, and that toothache turns into a dental emergency. A broader perspective might make a more tranquil course possible. You could spend time addressing smaller problems before they become disasters. But as the water keeps rolling, it is hard to think.

To calm the chaos, we need to think about how we'd like to spend our time. We need to think about any stretch of time before we are hurtling through it. We need time to pause in the calm shallows and think about what we need to do, and what we want to do.

This becomes even more important as time becomes more limited. I hear this all the time in my conversations with people who are building careers and raising families, such as Teresa Coda, a Tranquility by Tuesday participant. She and her husband moved back to her hometown in central Pennsylvania during the pandemic. Teresa's mother would provide what Teresa calls a "power hour" of childcare a few times a week for their two little girls, both under age three. With Teresa and her husband not wanting to expand their human-contact bubble beyond close family, they switched off workdays and used nap time to charge through their to-do lists.

The key to making this work for over a year was "being really clear about what I needed to get done, so I could take the best advantage of small chunks of time," Teresa says. When you have only an hour here and an hour there, "you have to go into those hours with the goal in mind. Or else an hour gets frittered away."

She began thinking this through, systematically, during a designated weekly planning time (Friday afternoons—for reasons we'll talk about in this chapter). She honed her list down to her most important tasks, professionally and personally. She would assign these tasks to particular days, and then, within the day, assign tasks to the slots when her husband or mother had the girls, and assign bonus tasks to times when everyone was likely to be sleeping.

None of this was easy. But as she built this habit, she found that she could be quite productive in the limited time she had. "If I have a clear goal in mind of what I want to work on for an hour, then I can make a lot of use of that hour," she says.

This is the goal of **Tranquility by Tuesday Rule 2: Plan on Fridays**.

As with giving yourself a bedtime, this rule is straightforward on a practical level. Each Friday, as Teresa started doing, and as I have been doing for years, you carve out twenty minutes to think about the upcoming Monday–Sunday week. What would you most like to do during that span of 168 hours? Which of the things that are already on your calendar are most important?

Since you are one person, with one life, it's most efficient to look at all of that life. So I'd recommend creating a three-category priority list for the upcoming week:

◆   Career
◆   Relationships
◆   Self

Write this list somewhere you'll be able to reference, such as in a planner. List a few items—no more than a handful—in each category. What would you most like to do, professionally? What would you like to do to nurture your relationships with friends, family, or community members? What would you like to do to advance your own health, spiritual development, or happiness?

I'm sure you have a great many things going on in your life, but the first part of this exercise should focus on those aspirations that would most make you feel like you'd had a wonderful week. For instance, career priorities might include a long-scheduled lunch with a former client, and designing the timeline for a big project. Relationship priorities might include calling a friend who's going through a tough time, and taking a teen whose school has

a random half-day out for lunch. Personal priorities might include a run on a new-to-you trail, and watching a concert of your
favorite Beethoven symphony that's being streamed on an orchestra's webpage. Mark time for these things on your calendar if
they aren't there already.

During this planning session, you should then also assess
what you need to do over the next week, even if these expectations don't rise to top priority status (and may be less fun). Look
at what is already on your calendar. Make sure you know all your
commitments for the next week, with a quick glance forward at
the next few weeks to be sure there's nothing massive you've forgotten about. What do you need to do to prepare? Are there logistics you need to figure out? Decide when you will make these
preparations, and note this on your calendar or in a planner. You
can strategize ways to ignore, minimize, or outsource anything
that you'd like to spend less time on. That meeting that has been
rescheduled four times already is unlikely to happen this week either, so go ahead and put it out of its misery by canceling it. Maybe
your assistant can handle that check-in phone call with the venue
hosting next month's big event.

After thinking about the upcoming workweek, I'd suggest
making a rough plan for the following weekend (not the Saturday–
Sunday that comes right after the Friday when you are doing this
planning, but the *next* one). Then take a minute or two to update
the plan for the immediately upcoming weekend, based on whatever new information or invitations have come in. If your life is
tightly entwined with someone else's, you can make a quick call

(or visit, if you're in the same place) to confirm anything requiring input or approval.

And that's . . . it. You figure out where you're going, and how to deal with any rough patches. You clear away things that aren't the best use of your time. Thinking about how you'd like to spend your hours vastly increases the chances of spending them in meaningful ways.

A powerful and easy habit

Friday planning is simple. Some people enjoy fancy planners, high-end pens, and washi tape. Some people like to make this session a treat, with a favorite beverage appropriate for the time of day, or a soaring movie soundtrack. All of those things are great; none of them are necessary. I use a notebook or a planner, and cross-reference with my calendar. Notes in an electronic calendar can work too.

The tool doesn't matter. What matters is that you do it.

If you do it, as Teresa discovered, Friday planning is powerful. It's certainly the best way I've found to calm the chaos, get more done, and have a shot at enjoying life. Indeed, if you find someone whose life logistics inspire the awe I once felt watching a circus act where eight motor bikes zoomed around inside a giant metal sphere simultaneously, I'd wager that person's planning game—even if done with professional assistance—is strong.

This rule to "Plan on Fridays" really encompasses two points: First, the value of a weekly planning session, and second, the value of planning on Fridays, specifically. The first is by far the most important, as I'll explain below, though I think choosing Fridays is really what makes this habit life-changing.

The case for planning life in weeks

Any designated weekly planning time can work. If you already have one that works, you don't have to change it! But if your life features any complexities at all, then you do need a designated weekly planning time. A week is the "unit of repeat" as mathematicians put it, in the pattern of our schedules, at least in any society where you're likely to be reading this book. A week is long enough to encompass actions beyond immediate crises, but also short enough for you to have a good sense of the landscape, and to be able to commit to times and actions with reasonable certainty.

If you've been planning in a more ad hoc manner, or barely planning at all, your first structured session—where you think about the whole week, and think about both professional and personal priorities—will produce some immediate benefits.

For starters, you might save time. If you see that you are meeting with the same people on Tuesday and Thursday, you might push to be efficient with the agenda and get through both matters in one meeting. That's an hour you've freed up, right there, that would have been lost if you'd just tromped from thing to thing.

More important, you will approach the week holistically, and this broader perspective can enable wiser choices. If you see that Tuesday is already full, and you've got something big due on Wednesday, you can carve out time on Monday for that assignment. This allows for a more tranquil approach to a deadline than the usual last-minute stress. If you would like to be at a kid's after-school baseball game on Thursday, and you see that a team whose meetings always run long is angling to meet on either Wednesday or Thursday afternoon, you know to push hard for the former. Life might not land as you wish. But in the absence of seeing the whole week at once, you won't know how much your answer matters.

This rule has a lot of upside given that it takes only twenty minutes. The real benefits, though, accrue over time when the session becomes a habit, and long-term life shaping becomes possible. For instance, during any given week:

- You can commit to intermediate steps toward larger goals, thus making larger goals feel more doable.
- You can start to anticipate bigger problems (or opportunities) and build in time to address them before they become emergencies.
- You can think ahead about what might be important to do, and put these things on your schedule, so that when you get to that week, the week's top priorities are already there, and the planning process becomes even quicker.

◆ You can think about potential future desires, and know that there is a way to send a message to Future You that will be received when Future You is capable of acting on it.

The first three benefits are worthwhile enough, but I think this last one—the ability to communicate with Future You—is really a superpower in a world where few people follow through on intentions.

Let's say you read about a professional award. You realize that one of your colleagues would be a perfect fit. You'd like to nominate him. But most likely, the reason you are hearing about the award is that it was just given. Applications for next year's version won't be available for months.

This thought could flit right out of your brain. But if you have a designated weekly planning time, you can write a note on your calendar for that time at some point in the future, perhaps a Friday afternoon three months before the award is given. You know that Future You will see that note when Future You is in planning mode. At that point, Future You—doing the weekly planning session that you always do—will remember the award and why your colleague should win it. Future You will look up the deadline and application process, and then make a plan to either do it as a priority over the next week, or assign it to a Friday planning time in a future week. Or Future You will decide not to do it. But at least Future You will be making an active choice, rather than forgetting until Future You sees news about the award and realizes the deadline has slipped by again.

Regular weekly planning means future desires can be effectively captured and pushed several steps closer to fulfillment. This is a process you can repeat with any sort of desire. When you see tulips in April, you can send a message to you, in October, to choose a time to plant the bulbs. When you hear that a hotel in a national park often sells out for the summer on the first day it is open for bookings, you can send a note to Future You slightly ahead of that booking day, and know you will be prepared to seize a slot.

With matters big and small, over time, you start to see that the future can be shaped. You can direct its course. This sense of control amid life's turbulence is the essence of tranquility. You have the ability to make what matters happen, even when the water is rough.

The case for Fridays

This rule—to create a designated weekly planning time—is essential for calming the chaos. *When* that session occurs depends on your personal preference. But if you don't already have a designated time, or you do but you've noticed some flaws with it, then this brings us to the second part of this rule: Plan on *Fridays*.

If you observe a typical Monday–Friday work or school schedule, then Friday, and particularly Friday afternoon, has four main upsides over some other leading planning-time contenders (Monday mornings or Sunday nights, judging by my surveys).

- **There's little opportunity cost**. It is hard to start anything new on Friday afternoons. Many of us are sliding toward the weekend at that point. If this time would otherwise be wasted counting the hours until it is acceptable to sign off, why not repurpose it for planning?

- **You can make Monday productive**. If you plan on Fridays, you can make full use of your Monday mornings. Many of us have more energy at the start of things than we do later on. Planning on Fridays allows you to use that Monday-morning energy for making progress on big projects, rather than using that energy to think about what Future You (who may have less vim and vigor than Monday Morning You) should be doing. As a side note, if you discover in your Friday planning that you need to make an appointment or set up a meeting, you can still do this during Friday's business hours, with all of Monday available to you if you need it. Whereas if you wait until Monday morning to plan, and realize then that you need to reach out to someone, you won't get the meeting on the schedule until late Monday at the earliest. Most likely it will be Tuesday or later.

- **You can upgrade your weekends**. I aim to think about weekends one week ahead. But if you don't do that—and I am well aware that many people don't relish planning their leisure time eight to nine days in advance—planning on Friday gives you a chance to look at the immediately upcoming weekend. You can make arrangements for any family or social activities. You'll be more likely to make space for big adventures if you think about Saturday on Friday, rather than if you attempt to make a plan on Saturday morning when no one feels like doing much of anything.

♦ **You can calm the "Sunday scaries."** I know that a great many people plan on Sunday nights, and this does still allow for directing Monday-morning energy (sort of . . . if you find you need to collaborate with someone, you are less likely to get a response on Sunday evening than on Friday, and if you discover you need to make an appointment somewhere with business hours, you'll have to do that task on high-opportunity-cost Monday, instead of low-opportunity-cost Friday). But the big problem with planning on Sunday is that you go into the weekend without a plan for the upcoming workweek. You know there are complicated problems waiting for you, but you don't know exactly what. You don't know what you'll do to deal with these issues. This uncertainty can keep your brain churning through these questions. This is the big reason that even people who like their jobs can suffer from Sunday anxiety. They spend what could be leisure or family time mulling over the undefined tasks they'll face during the week ahead. If you know exactly how you plan to accomplish what you need to accomplish before you quit on Friday afternoon, then you can relax. You can give your brain a true break.

Do your weekly planning on Friday afternoon, Friday after Friday, and life will feel a lot more tranquil—on every day of the week.

From "what's happening" to "what's important"

Many of the Tranquility by Tuesday participants—like Teresa—were well versed with the idea of looking at their upcoming schedules. As busy professionals raising families, they lived by their calendars. But for many, this shift from "what's happening" to "what's important"—and broadening planning from meeting times to relationships and personal fulfillment—was intriguing. Indeed, some even found it exciting.

"I already do a weekly planning session for my work priorities. However, I see value in planning priorities in relationship and personal categories so that I don't feel like I did 'nothing' over the weekend," one person wrote. She began brainstorming all the new fun she could actively plan into her life. "I may be able to catch up with friends via Skype or with my husband during a weekday lunch in a restaurant's heated tent. I may be able to plan time for more ukulele practice, or plan my reading list, or plan a new workout routine."

People anticipated feeling a sense of calm, and a sense of progress.

Participant perspectives: Identifying obstacles

I asked participants to anticipate any challenges they might face in building a Friday planning habit.

A few folks worried that something could come up during their scheduled planning time, which can happen, but you can always create a back-up slot (as we'll learn about with Rule 5). While your first choice for your Friday planning session might be after lunch, if your boss unexpectedly asks to meet then, you could also plan right before leaving the office. Your third choice might be Friday morning because you have looked ahead and seen that the entire afternoon is booked.

Some people worried about forgetting, which is a problem that can be solved by setting an alarm or other such reminder, or by putting planning on Friday's daily task list.

In general, though, taking twenty minutes out of 168 hours to plan the other 167.67 hours seems like a reasonable ask. So the most common challenges people anticipated were psychological, rather than logistical.

Some people worried about being too tired or distracted on Friday afternoon, or feeling rushed to get to undone work before the weekend. If that's the case, and you worry about pausing for twenty minutes, try planning for ten. Something is almost always better than nothing, and in even a few minutes you might find a way to keep yourself from having piles of undone work on Friday afternoon *next week*. As for feeling tired and distracted, remember that planning work takes less energy than actually doing the tasks you're planning. It is far easier to write "call three prospective clients" in a planner than to actually call those clients. That Friday-afternoon fatigue is precisely why this is a good time for planning.

A few folks appealed to the muse of spontaneity, worrying that planning would make life feel less fun. I've seen this complaint frequently in other contexts, but because I instructed people to plan relationship and personal priorities—which were generally things people wanted to do—this dialed down the grumbles. Getting tickets with a friend to see your favorite sports team play inspires far less resistance than planning when you need to clean out the garage.

The more affecting concern was that some folks felt the stream was rolling so swiftly that there was no point even trying to row:

- "Sometimes I feel so overwhelmed by the amount of work I have to do that I don't even want to write it down. I am a little worried that creating a monster list of what needs to happen will feel demoralizing."
- "When life is overwhelming I stop this planning practice, because I don't 'have time.' I can't see beyond the

urgent task in front of me; there is no space between my thoughts, they're swirling around together."

We have all been there, struggling through days when we feel like we're drowning. When we feel this way, though, I would argue that a twenty-minute planning session can function as a life preserver. The mass of obligations is going to be the same whether you've thought through them or not, but undefined expectations are scarier than known ones. When we know what we are facing, we have something to hold on to. We can prepare ourselves and manage our energy. A sense of being overwhelmed is a sign that planning is even *more* necessary, rather than a reason to skip the practice.

Finally, there were a few folks who felt that life was truly unpredictable. "I get frustrated when I plan well but then the plan gets torpedoed. It makes me not want to waste the time," one person wrote.

That is understandable, and more so in recent years than if I had written this book five years ago. Tranquility by Tuesday participants were just emerging from a year of pandemic restrictions. They had seen many plans for 2020 go up in smoke, from international vacations to professional conferences to milestones such as a child's first sleep-away camp. Enough cancellations and you can wonder why you bother. Why not spend potential planning time relaxing and just take life as it comes?

It is a tempting argument. But even in an uncertain world, there are reasons for planning:

1. Many plans *don't* have to change.

Let's say you set six major intentions for the week, and a sudden change in circumstances means that two just can't happen. This is frustrating, but the good news is that you've still made progress on four. This is far better than zero. In life, all-or-nothing thinking is seldom helpful. Wise people do not let disappointment in one matter keep them from enjoying everything else that's going right.

2. Many wonderful things absolutely won't happen without planning.

Let's say that someday you'd like to go back to school to get that degree, learn to paint and enter your work in an art show, or take your extended family on a trip to New Zealand. Even if a pandemic derailed these options for a year, and who knows what else will in the future, they won't fall like fairy dust into anyone's life. You have to actively plan to make them happen. Time is always a gamble. We have to take our chances if we want these things in our obituaries.

3. Plans have benefits even when the plans don't happen.

There is a famous quote from Dwight Eisenhower (who himself called it a statement he had heard long before in the army) that "Plans are worthless, but planning is everything." In a normal life context, just as on the battlefield, things seldom go exactly as planned. However, when you have thought through the logistics, you can pivot more easily than if you've never even pondered the possibilities.

When we are thinking of pleasurable plans, as opposed to military campaigns, there's an even better argument for planning: **anticipation accounts for the bulk of any happiness associated with an event**. If I have made a reservation at The French Laundry for a date in August (something that turns out to require being on the reservation system right when it opens months before), I will spend much time before August looking forward to this culinary perfection. I will think about my truffles, my wine, even the provenance of the butter on my bread. I will think about my upcoming pleasure for far longer than the three hours the meal itself will take. I would certainly like the meal to happen. But even if the meal itself *didn't* happen, my plans would have produced a lot of joy. In a world that can feel cold and difficult, this sense of anticipation isn't nothing. Indeed, it is sometimes what makes us willing to get out of bed.

The results

In general, plans do happen. Certainly, the Tranquility by Tuesday participants' plans did. By the end of the second week of the study, considerably more people reported spending time on their personal and professional priorities than had reported recent progress on their priorities before the program began.

Progress is motivational, so perhaps it's not surprising that this rule had one of the highest rule-adherence scores of any in the study. At the end of nine weeks, the mean score on a 1 to 7 point scale for whether people intended to continue planning at a designated time each week was north of 6.

As with Eisenhower's understanding that plans allow you to pivot well, my participants found that planning helped them deal with what they hadn't planned for. One person wrote that "I knew what to expect, and also knew when I could pivot when a time-sensitive client assignment popped up unexpectedly." Another person wrote that "I had a clear view on what was important and urgent this week. In consequence, I had more freedom to react to unforeseen situations." This person wound up needing to change a lot from the original plan. But she had thought through what was expendable and what was not, and so, "when having to deviate from the plans, I had the security to not lose anything absolutely necessary from view."

This certainty that the important things wouldn't get dropped—"maintaining forward progress, despite disruptions," as one person put it—created a sense of tranquility, even as life pitched all sorts of rocks and rapids at the study participants. Dozens of responses described this sense of calm after just *one week* using a structured, priority-focused planning session:

- ◆ "[Planning] helped me feel steady during a very busy week. This month is the highest workload of my year, and I'm handling the stress well."
- ◆ "[This rule] made a busy week less chaotic, and ensured I spent time doing things I wanted to do as well as things I needed to do."
- ◆ "I felt like I did enough even if I didn't finish everything, because I did what I planned to do."

When you see the whole week, and everything that's going on, you start to have a better sense of what fits, and what will not fit. "I found it easier to say 'no' to unimportant things because my week was already planned out, and full," one person said. "I didn't have any big project or activity that I got to the end of the week and said 'I just couldn't get to that this week,' which felt great."

Developing the skill of making reasonable to-do lists is no small thing. Checking in every Friday provides accountability. If you keep declaring something a priority for the upcoming week, and you keep not doing it, eventually you are going to have to acknowledge that.

Perhaps you will decide to let it go. Or—and this happened for many project participants—you will decide to make it happen. Multiple people reported making progress on bigger projects, the sort of projects that had often been pushed off in the past.

"Planning helped get me out of the twenty-four-hour mindset

and into a more long-term, slow outlook of my goals," one person wrote.

Another made a big career move: "One of my professional priorities was to apply for a new job at my organization, and this made it easier to spend three evenings plus extra time on the weekend preparing my cover letter and resume."

One reported that "The best part of the planning for me was that I came up with a list of concrete, well-articulated mini-steps that are part of a big amorphous project, and I mapped a few mini-steps into a prescheduled block of deep work time each day. Then I actually got them done!"

For many, planning helped create these blocks of time for focused work, as people looked at their schedules strategically. They rescheduled meetings that were dangling in the middle of otherwise open hours, or made mindful choices, such as tackling real work, instead of processing email, during an open hour before a 10 a.m. meeting.

If work felt more calm, personal time felt more joyful.

"By thinking ahead, I planned some fun stuff: a park play-date with another family, an outdoor moms-only happy hour, and getting carry-out from our local parish fish fry," one woman wrote. "That's a pretty good amount of fun stuff during a busy work/school week and I got to experience the joy of anticipation and the joy of actually doing these fun things."

Working out the rough patches

Of course, all did not go perfectly. While COVID-19 restrictions were easing in the United States during the spring of 2021, some international respondents had gone into new lockdowns that complicated their plans. However, a good plan can make life feel doable even in a scenario when, for instance, daycares and schools are suddenly shut down. When you know your most important work priorities, and what absolutely has to happen, you do these things first in any time that becomes available. Much doesn't get done, but what does get done is what should get done.

A few folks made the in-retrospect-obvious discovery that if you make a plan, you have to keep looking at the plan if you want that plan to inform your decisions (this is one reason I keep my planner open on my desk, which is in my home office, and thus visible on weekends too). One respondent reported tucking the plan somewhere, where it was promptly forgotten until the next Friday.

"It's a bit like budgeting beforehand and then not looking at your budget until your money is gone," this person rued. "I have to make reviewing my plan daily a habit."

Other people discovered—or rediscovered—that planning involves time estimation, and time estimation is hard. My general rule is that most things take longer than you think they will. That means planning less per day than you think will fit. A five-item to-do list can happen. A fifty-item to-do list? Not so much. That

said, it's possible to become better at estimation with time tracking, and crowdsourcing estimates for anything that seems unclear.

Planning, in general, gets easier with practice. You figure out
what must be tightly planned, and what can be more freeform,
with the balance varying in different circumstances. One person
reflected that "I don't think I planned my week as well as I could
have last Friday. I identified key professional, personal, and rela-
tional priorities, but I didn't time block them and so while I knew
that I wanted to get them done (and I did), there were still many
moments throughout the week when I thought 'what should I be
doing right now?' Since part of the purpose of this strategy is to
eliminate ambiguity about how time should be spent (at least as
far as I see it), having a more concrete plan would be useful."

Some chaos takes time to unwind. One participant lamented
that, especially at work, the urgent and important things tended
to crowd out the important but not urgent things. There did not
seem to be enough space in any given week to get to both. But
perhaps, with baby steps, eventually there would be. "Even half
an hour and just starting to think about something is better than
just having it on the list and never getting started. I hope that
keeping on planning my weeks will also make this easier. The
important things that are not urgent yet will become urgent
sooner or later (most of the time) and if I started working on
them soon enough then there won't be as much to do at a later
time, which in turn opens up more space for the important but
not (yet) urgent things."

As this person anticipated, the benefits of planning build

as you keep doing it. You keep assessing what's going on, and looking at the future. The important stuff has a fighting chance of happening before it becomes urgent. You build the critical-thinking capacity for figuring out potential problems before they happen, and the agency to rally your resources to solve the problems that can be solved. This means there are fewer crises, and those that happen don't become disasters.

A twenty-minute Friday planning session doesn't solve everything. But I promise that it does solve a lot. So why not at least experiment? One Tranquility by Tuesday participant was unconvinced of the wisdom, but when asked how she would address this challenge, she wrote that "I can join a time study where I'm directly asked to do this whether I like it or not."

I love this answer. We all want a better relationship with time, even as we sense that ever-rolling stream Isaac Watts wrote about bearing our years on by. There's no harm in, as the design thinkers say, trying stuff. Maybe it won't work. But maybe, in twenty minutes on Fridays, you will be able to create a sense of calm and happiness. You will make time for what matters. And that can make floating on the ever-rolling stream a far more pleasant experience.

Take the next step

◆

MAKE A LIST OF 100 DREAMS

To plan our upcoming 168 hours with an eye toward what's important, and not just what's happening, we need to know what is important. Perhaps you already know every single thing you'd like to do with your time. That is wonderful. But sometimes this is less clear. I am reminded of the trouble with that graduation cliché to "follow your passion." This requires knowing your passion. How many people know this for sure at age 22? Or even 43 or 65? Passions can shift as our circumstances shift too.

Figuring out what you want to spend time doing takes work. It is also worthwhile work. Dreaming is productive. When we know what deserves space in life, we can plan with a focus on pleasure and meaning.

To figure out what deserves more time in your life, I suggest making something called a List of 100 Dreams. This exercise was shared with me by career coach Caroline Ceniza-Levine more than a dozen years ago. I wrote about it in my first time-management book, *168 Hours*, and I continue to hear from people more than a decade later about how helpful it is.

The List of 100 Dreams is exactly what you think it would be. You write down a hundred things you'd like to experience or have in your life. These can be regular bucket-list items (Visit Fiji! Run a marathon!) but most people's bucket lists stop around item #25 when they've listed the twenty-five countries they want to visit. Getting to a hundred is hard. This is the point. You start thinking beyond the Fiji trip, and start thinking of more off-beat items (getting the house professionally decorated for Christmas?).

I suggest splitting the list into the same three categories we talked about for Friday planning: career, relationships, self.

The List of 100 Dreams is not a to-do list. You are not holding yourself to any of this. So don't edit your ideas. You can absolutely write "sing in Carnegie Hall" even if you've never sung anything other than "Happy Birthday" at kid parties. Writing that might spur you to put "take voice lessons" as the next item. And then "Join Joan and Robert the next time they go to a karaoke bar" as the item after that. Only ninety-seven to go!

You will need to come back to this list several times. Some items may never happen. That's fine. But hopefully, by the time you get to a hundred, you will have plenty of doable aspirations, both professionally and personally. These can provide fodder for your planning sessions. If you think it would be fun to visit a local beer garden, you can reach out to a friend and make a plan to meet there next Thursday. This becomes a relationship priority for the upcoming week. If you think it might be helpful for your career to form a small mastermind group, you can spend time over the next week thinking about who might join and what structure would work.

The deeper concept here is to really think about what might be enjoyable. During the busy years, many of us assume we have no time, and so we don't bother to think about what we'd do with time if we had it. That ensures that when discretionary time does appear—as it does for everyone, at least occasionally—we do whatever is right in front of us. We spend the evening sorting the mail pile instead of asking Joan and Robert for the karaoke schedule, swapping off kid coverage with our partners, and heading out for some Tuesday-night tunes.

Tuesday will pass one way or another. All time is eventually just water under the bridge. But thinking about how we'd like to spend future time can nudge the course of the stream toward something more fun, or at least more memorable. The List of 100 Dreams will do just that. So take a little time to get started, and you'll reap the rewards for years to come.

Your turn

◆

PLAN ON FRIDAYS

Planning questions:

1. What does your planning look like now?

2. This rule is about creating a designated weekly planning time. What day will you plan each week?

3. When will you plan? Feel free to choose a clock time (2 p.m.) or an event time (during the baby's nap; after my staff meeting).

4. How much time, in minutes, do you think it will take to plan the week?

5. What benefits do you think you would see (or do you see) from a designated weekly planning time?

6. What obstacles might keep you from a regular planning practice?

7. How can you address these challenges?

Implementation questions:

1. How did planning on Friday (or your chosen planning day) affect your week?

2. Describe any challenges you faced while implementing this week's strategy.

3. How did you deal with these challenges?

4. Did you need to modify this rule? If so, how?

5. How likely are you to continue using this rule in your life?

Move by 3 p.m.

Exercise doesn't take time, it makes time.

A few years ago, I gave a talk at a rather vast corporate campus. Teams aimed to cluster together, but as you might imagine with a big organization, this did not always happen. One woman told me that she had recently started working with a group located several buildings away. This meant that at least once or twice a day, she had to hike across campus for meetings. Since she was usually trying to finish something beforehand, these were brisk strolls.

It could have been exhausting, and indeed, she was sharing this situation as an example of a time management challenge. But, almost as an afterthought, she mentioned that this forced daily activity had upsides. She was arriving at these meetings feeling far more alert than most people do in the middle of the workday. Some chronic stiffness she'd been living with had gotten better. She had suspected that moving her body more might help on that front. It just never fit into her schedule.

Until it did.

Her comment stayed with me because it hits on such a prevalent modern problem. The human body was built to move. For much of human history, people had to move all the time. But if you are reading this book, you probably spend much of the workday sitting. Days off might feature more activity—but they also might not. Most of us drive most places. The COVID-19 pandemic exacerbated this problem as millions of people began working from home, shuffling a few feet from bed to desk, and getting as many groceries and household items delivered as possible. Delivery professionals scored lots of steps. The rest of us? Not really.

Our sedentary lives are nice as progress goes—I'd rather spend my days writing than fetching water—but there is a tipping point where productivity starts to suffer. I keep a running collection (pun intended) of studies comparing physical activity to various pharmaceuticals, particularly those prescribed for the chronic conditions that can sap people's energy. Regular exercise turns out to be as effective as antidepressants for mild to moderate depression. Exercise works as well as sleeping pills on mild insomnia. One study found that people who walked briskly five times or more over a seven-day period were 60 percent less sensitive to pain than a control group by the end of the week.

Exercise is also a natural stimulant. One of my favorite

studies of people's energy levels through the day found that a five-minute burst of physical activity, wedged in when people felt particularly weary, boosted self-reported energy scores from a 3 to a 9 on a 10-point scale. An hour later, people still gave themselves a 6, which is double where they'd been before.

It does not require a huge leap in logic to imagine that people got more done during the fifty-five minutes when their energy levels hovered north of 6 than they would have gotten done in a full hour, or maybe even more time, stuck at 3. Because of this, I like to say that exercise (like sleep) doesn't take time. It *makes* time. Within reason, time devoted to physical activity will be paid back to you as you are better able to focus, to make good choices with time, and to handle challenges as they arise. Moving our bodies is simply a great way to get more done.

The trouble is that while people might agree with this assessment, "exercise," as we perceive it, doesn't fit easily into modern life. The woman who had to hike ten minutes to meet with her team woke up early to drive to work, worked a full day, then drove home to her household responsibilities. When exercise means an hour-long gym session requiring a shower afterward, few people with full-time jobs and families will do this more than a few times per week. That is fine (see the next chapter on Tranquility by Tuesday Rule 4: Three times a week is a habit) but if we're looking for the mood- and energy-boosting effects of activity, daily is better. That's the dosing schedule for the pharmaceuticals prescribed for the chronic conditions that exercise can alleviate. So that's the dose we're aiming for.

That brings me to **Tranquility by Tuesday Rule 3: Move by 3 p.m.**

To boost energy, and to make life feel more doable, commit to doing some form of physical activity for **at least ten minutes in the first half of every single day**. More is better. But ten minutes is a start. Even ten minutes can change a day, as many Tranquility by Tuesday participants found, and changing days is how we ultimately change our lives.

The "move" part of this rule can be any sort of movement. Most people walk, but push-ups, sit-ups, jumping jacks, kettlebell swings, and so forth, are options. Chasing kids around the yard or pushing a stroller counts. Traditional exercise such as running or a fitness class is wonderful if it works, but if it doesn't, there's no need to get sweaty enough to require a shower afterward. The lady who shared her schedule challenge at my talk wasn't changing clothes before her meetings and she still saw benefits. Something is always better than nothing.

The "before 3 p.m." part requires a little more explanation. Some research has found that people who exercise regularly are more likely to do so in the morning—because, as we discussed in the morning routine section, mornings tend to be more regimented in people's lives. If you build exercise into your morning routine, it will happen, whereas a planned 5 p.m. workout might be foiled by a meeting that runs late or a kid needing a ride home.

Yet you'll notice I didn't say "move by 10 a.m." My intention with this rule is not to persuade people to sign up for a 6 a.m. CrossFit session. If you decide to do that, or you are already a dedicated morning exerciser, great—the energy boost from that decision will pay dividends all day long. However, if your preferred mode of exercise is a date with your treadmill at 8 p.m. most nights after your kids go to bed, there's no need to change that, and indeed, I would congratulate you on using a time of day that many people have trouble turning to productive ends.

Instead, my point is that unless you already exercise all seven days of the week, 365 days a year, then this rule will nudge you to fit a bit more activity into your life—and generally in situations where a bit more activity would be a very good thing.

The strategy of a daily habit

A rule to move by 3 p.m. leads to a few positive outcomes, especially on busy weekdays. First, unless you did manage to squeeze in that 6 a.m. workout, this rule means you will need to take at least one break. Everyone needs breaks. It is easy to get sucked into back-to-back meetings or appointments, filling the space between them with email checks. When we don't take real breaks, though, we take fake ones, which explains how you lost forty-five minutes the other day looking through photos of a high school classmate's dog on social media and then clicking on ads for stylish pajamas. A ten-minute walk break would have been more efficient.

As for 3 p.m., this time is not random. When people track

their energy levels through the day, this is roughly the point when they hit their nadir, on average, at least during regular business hours. So as a second benefit, if you know that you need to move by 3 p.m., and you haven't gotten to it until that point, a little microburst here can get you back on track. Most likely you'll be able to power through the rest of the workday without relying on caffeine or candy bars.

But this rule, like all of them, has a deeper purpose.

To ensure that you move by 3 p.m. daily, especially in our sedentary society, you have to think through your days. You have to think about each day's landscape—both workdays and days off—and where there might be spots of usable time. You become a general, surveying the battlefield. What can move? What can't? What logistical problems must be solved as you march through your hours?

This strategic mindset has all sorts of spillover benefits. If you can spot the space, or create the space, for a ten-minute walk, what else can you engineer? It might be more than you thought. Fundamentally, **you are in charge of your time**. A daily ten-minute break is a reminder of this truth, and a nudge to expand this scope of authority as you can. Committing to this rule provides daily evidence of the autonomy you have over your life, and over time, this daily evidence can change a narrative of being overwhelmed.

Committing to move by 3 p.m. also nudges you to pay attention to how your energy ebbs and flows during the day, and the control you can exercise over your energy levels. When you understand these rhythms, you can start planning your days with these rhythms in mind. You plan the tough stuff for when you are best able to handle it. You figure out how to strategically deploy little bursts of activity to rally through the low moments. In short, you become like an elite athlete's trainer, coaxing out peak performance. This mindset shift toward optimization lets you accomplish more than you might have thought possible.

To be sure, ten minutes isn't much, and perhaps it sounds silly to be evoking generals and trainers when you're just walking around the block. But this rule is really about creating a new mindset about yourself and your hours. Plus, moving tends to feel good, at least once you're in motion. As your energy levels rise, you'll start looking for other places in your schedule to move. You'll likely stretch that ten-minute allotment, at least some of the time. A quick 2:30 p.m. walk, done out of duty, will bring you out into a jewel of a June day. The big blue sky will seem to be smiling. You'll wind up walking for forty minutes as you realize there is nothing that can't wait.

Participant perspectives: Ideas for implementation

Most Tranquility by Tuesday participants already exercised regularly. About 60 percent reported exercising at least two hours a week (the equivalent of four thirty-minute sessions) and only 3 percent reported doing none. People exercised in both common and not-so-common ways, including bike commutes and stacking wood. As the world emerged from the pandemic in the spring of 2021, few people reported going to the gym, but a number had invested in Peloton bikes, or at least used the app.

Still, despite this already enviable level of activity, most people were willing and excited to find more time, particularly in the crevices of the day, and particularly with this mindset that exercise could be a productivity tool, and not a chore done out of some vague desire to lose weight. Only 7.5 percent of participants claimed this rule wouldn't work for them.

They offered all kinds of ideas for when they could move.

"I could make a rule to go for a ten-minute walk after every meeting (or meeting block if I have a few back to back)," one person wrote. "I feel like my head is always swimming when I get out of a meeting and I need a break from the screen at that time anyway to gather my thoughts."

Several suggested walking while on audio-only work calls, or during virtual meetings when it was OK to turn the camera off. A few dog owners who worked from home suggested that they could walk their pets during the workday, instead of just opening the back door. With my data collected during spring, some liked the idea of ditching the car for short walks to school or daycare as the weather warmed. One person used the nudge of this rule to restart an old habit of jumping on the treadmill for five minutes at a time, particularly with the incline bumped up. And one parent aimed for a walking date with an eighth grader when the teen finished virtual school each day.

People also spotted opportunities to turn up the intensity on normal activities. One person decided to be more intentional about running around in the yard with the kids when they were out on their bikes in the middle of the day, and another decided to tackle the pile of dead branches left over from a recent ice storm.

Participant perspectives: Identifying obstacles

Of course, alongside the ideas, people foresaw plenty of challenges—both anticipated and in the actual implementation of this rule. Some people have inflexible jobs that preclude movement, or at least chosen movement. One person noted that her contract required that she stay in the building during her shift, and that she had only twenty minutes for lunch daily at an assigned time. Fortunately, she was done by 3:30 p.m. each day, and she enjoyed a relaxing walk at that point—which isn't too far removed from 3 p.m. For folks with strictly contracted hours that involve two fifteen-minute breaks and a thirty-minute lunch, it might be possible to use one of those breaks to walk around outside. (Unless your job involves, say, chopping wood. Then you should feel free to skip this chapter.)

For some people, the workday just felt too busy to build in a consciously chosen break. Some people feared coworker judgement if they appeared to have the time to do anything other than keep their heads down. One person described this challenge as "Telling myself the story that I don't have time and have more urgent/important things to do, and worrying what my coworkers will think if I go for a mid-afternoon walk."

A looming deadline can make ten minutes feel too precious to squander, even if we know, on some level, that those minutes might enable hours of more focused work. Other people's demands can feel incessant; one person described this frenzy as "the seemingly constant incoming nonsense." Even if we're not physically chained to our desks, exerting obvious authority over our time—which is what leaving and going for a walk entails—can feel risky in an environment where busyness is prized.

While the lack of coworker stares might make home-office breaks feel more doable, several of my work-from-home respondents told me that they were still supervising young children whose childcare arrangements or school schedules had been disrupted by the pandemic. As one woman wrote, she might theoretically be able to jump on the treadmill during nap time, but "12:30–2:30 p.m. nap time is one of my primary work slots." When her husband came home at 3 p.m. and took over, she needed to finish the work she hadn't gotten done before. She had to fight the narrative in her brain that a ten-minute walk break was just hopelessly indulgent. (My advice: No need to use nap time! A stroller walk is a nice long way to keep a toddler contained.)

A few people mentioned the practical concern that exercise might make them sweaty.

"If I do anything that really raises a sweat I would have to change first, and then after, which takes walking to the bathroom on the other side of the building," one person wrote, doing the calculation that this would add ten minutes on either side of a ten-minute workout. That would definitely raise the stakes on this rule—mentally tripling the amount of time something takes is a handy way to talk yourself out of almost anything—but if you don't feel the need to change clothes after walking from the parking lot to your desk, it's hard to see that a few more minutes of the same activity would be much different.

People mentioned the day getting away from them, or being unmotivated, either because of specific factors like weather, or in general: "I overestimate the burden, and underestimate the benefit, of small bits of activity."

We can see the errors in our thinking, and yet we still succumb to these excuses in the moment. People anticipated being tired. Or they were good about moving during the week, but everything fell apart during unstructured weekends. With limited free time, some people preferred to do other things (e.g., read) during small breaks between work commitments.

Participant perspectives: Creatively overcoming challenges

With a little thought, people found ways to solve these challenges. For instance, the person concerned about what colleagues might think decided to just "do it anyway. I don't always go for a walk mid-afternoon at work, but on days when I do, I am more productive the rest of the day, and nothing goes wrong in the ten minutes I'm away from my desk."

People who didn't have childcare involved the kids. One person reported doing yoga with a toddler planted firmly in the middle of her yoga mat. A slightly older child might enjoy his own yoga mat and a video aimed at younger viewers. A five-minute dance party to a catchy tune can completely change the mood when little ones are headed into meltdown mode. It can change the mood when *you* are headed into meltdown mode as well.

Some people began repurposing breaks they were already taking; one devotee of the Pomodoro technique (working for twenty-five minutes, then taking a five-minute break) figured out that the Peloton app "has tiny workouts (five or ten minutes) that I've been sneaking in during my Pomodoro breaks."

A few folks who had trouble remembering to move by 3 p.m. started adding a walk break as a daily recurring to-do, or began scheduling breaks as they would meetings. Some participants discovered the wisdom of creating a menu of options. A daily thirty-minute lunchtime walk in sunny seventy-five-degree weather was the ideal, but if the forecast called for thunderstorms they could walk up and down the stairs at the office, or close the door and do some push-ups, or even decide to take a longer break on foul-weather days and head to an indoor gym.

Others decided to explore their resistance. Much of this turned out to be all-or-nothing thinking—that anything less than an hour at the gym didn't count as exercise, or that unless they were drenched with sweat (necessitating that ten-minute change before and after) it was all worthless. One person wrote of realizing "that it can be something as simple as just walking for ten minutes. I think the main thing I need to do is to redefine exercise to feel less resistance and dread to do it."

One participant even began repeating this mantra: "Only ten minutes and whatever exercise I want to." No sprints dished out by the gym teacher as punishment. No climbing a rope. No silly-looking clothes. No counting calories burned as atonement for food choices. The focus can be solely on pleasure.

With a flexible mindset, I maintain that there is always a way to do at least ten minutes of *something*. In the glow afterward, you'll see that there's also always a reason to get moving. I certainly found this when I decided, a few years ago, to run at least a mile every day. Some days during my three-year streak I wound up running little laps in tiny hotel rooms, which felt ridiculous, as did running slow circles in my basement when I was nine months pregnant. But all of this did in fact make me feel better afterward. Not as good as, say, running five miles along a cliff-top overlooking the ocean, but better. One Tranquility by Tuesday respondent traveled to visit her brother, who had just been diagnosed with cancer, during the week that participants experimented with this rule. It would have been an understandable reason to skip the week, but she decided that there might be real upsides to the happiness boost. And so, "I dealt with feet sliding on the rug because I don't have a mat here," she said. "I used a Le

Creuset pot because my brother doesn't have light free weights. I found a big hill to walk and brought my brother with me. There's ALWAYS a way to exercise."

The results

With this problem-solving mindset, and a focus on pleasure, most people saw benefits from moving every single day by 3 p.m. Tranquility by Tuesday participants saw a steady increase in their sense of having enough energy for what they needed or wanted to do over the course of the project. Initial agreement scores for the statement "Yesterday I had enough energy to handle my responsibilities" averaged 4.95 on my scale of 1 to 7.

After people implemented the rule about giving themselves a bedtime, agreement scores for the question of whether people had enough energy during the week for the things they wanted to do averaged 5.10. After people began moving by 3 p.m., agreement scores for the question of whether people had enough energy to handle their responsibilities during the week rose to 5.31. They kept rising before settling a bit, but even one month after the project ended, scores stayed elevated, with an average rating of 5.49 (for the question of whether people had enough energy to handle their responsibilities "yesterday"). This is a statistically significant rise, even for people who were already exercising, on average, pretty often. About 20 percent of the people in my study moved all the way from disagreeing that they had enough energy for their busy lives to agreeing that they had enough energy— over the course of nine weeks.

A few folks did decide to become morning exercisers, with all the upsides that keep people setting an alarm clock:

- "Whenever I get exercise early (especially first thing in the morning) that sense of accomplishment stays with me throughout the day, and gives me a sense of forward momentum."
- "It's all done for the day! It can't get derailed!"
- "Exercising in the morning allowed me to shower and get dressed in the morning (vs. some other undefined point in the day), so I felt better about myself when I ran a quick errand or walked up to the school to pick up my kids in the afternoon."

Those who focused more on the "before 3 p.m." part saw benefits from forcing space into the day. When we take a strategic approach to the day's hours, we can find a rhythm that works for us—alternating periods of focused work with real rejuvenation. Being away from the desk and the screen "creates an entire shift in mindset and attitude," one person wrote. Wrote another, "it was a nice mental break. I came back to my desk energized." People wrote of feeling "more calm and present" and "refreshed and focused" with "some perspective on workload."

"I definitely saw an increase in my mood and energy," one

respondent said. "It was just a hard week for many reasons and I didn't feel like moving most days but I knew if I did, I would feel better."

This reliability is what makes this rule magic. People spend a lot of time and money trying to make themselves feel more happy and alert. Ten minutes of physical activity will achieve that goal almost every time, and will do so for free. Indeed, these quick breaks often wound up becoming the highlights of people's days.

"Walking to the bakery in the next neighborhood in the sunshine with a band playing in the park was one of the best times I've had in ages," one person wrote, saying it was "great for my mental health."

As people stuck with this rule, they began to see the I-am-in-charge-of-my-time thinking that this rule encourages, and they began leaning into the day-by-day approach that makes lifelong habits possible.

"I think I was trying to find a time that would work every day instead of taking each day on its own and asking 'when does it work to go for a walk today?'" one person reported.

When we decide to do something every single day, we stop worrying about motivation, or whether some days will present extra challenges, or if the schedule will change. We just do it. This is a breakthrough in mindset. Asking "when?" instead of "if?" turns time in general into a problem-solving exercise. There is an answer. We just have to find it. And when we do, we'll return more focused, ready to do things that seemed hard before.

Take the next step

◆

GO OUTSIDE FOR TWENTY MINUTES A DAY

Daily physical activity can help calm the chaos, but it's not the only habit that can make life feel more joyful—and doable.

When Luke Bushatz returned from his deployment with the U.S. Army in Afghanistan, "he was really in crisis," his wife, Amy Bushatz, reports. He had suffered a traumatic brain injury when his vehicle was hit by an improvised explosive device. The attack killed several of his friends. Luke came back to the United States coping with post-traumatic stress and memory problems. Life for the family was difficult. But Amy noticed something. When they spent time outside, things seemed to get better. "It was easier to communicate with each other," she says. "He was more relaxed. It was like watching someone take a heavy backpack off over time."

Naturally, they began spending more time hiking and camping with their two young boys. In 2016 they decided to move to the little town of Palmer, Alaska, for better access to the outdoors. Luke loved it, eventually choosing a post-service career leading a nonprofit devoted to taking veterans into the backcountry. Amy was more mixed. Alaska is . . . Alaska. It's cold. And at times very dark. "I found that I was going outside and using this tool I had gifted myself with only when the weather pleased me," Amy says. "Living near nature, and having all the access in the world does you no good if you don't actually use it."

This realization led Amy to ask herself this question: What would happen if she made a habit of spending some time outside every day for a year?

She settled on at least twenty minutes a day—a time that seemed manageable, but also worthwhile if she was going to bother getting into her mittens, boots, balaclavas, and other cold-weather gear.

So that is what she did. Summer in Alaska is beautiful. Spring and fall feature glorious color, and since the Bushatz family bought a hot tub, even frosty days could feel celebratory. The dead of winter, though, turned out to be something altogether different. From November to January, the sun rises for just a few hours each day. One particularly memorable Palmer weather forecast was negative 20 degrees with a driving wind off the nearby glacier. "That was cold," Amy says. "Your nose hairs freeze. That is one weird feeling." In an effort to try new things with her outdoor time, she made the somewhat foolish decision to attempt a marathon in minus-ten-degree weather. Bordering on the edge of hypothermia, she had to bail at mile eighteen. In the course of her daily outdoor time she once almost bumped into a moose while scrolling around on her phone.

But, even on the hard days, she always came back inside feeling better. She made it through 365 days, and then she kept going. She had recently crossed 1,400-plus consecutive days when we talked. "I cannot emphasize the breadth of mental health benefits enough," she says. "Not just emotional health, but creativity, and mentally being able to have better relationships with family and friends." Every day there is a reason to step away from her computer for a while and to appreciate the wonders of the world, even if that's the wonders of the parking lot outside an airport, if that's the only twenty minutes that will work.

I love this idea. Once you've started moving every day by 3 p.m., why not commit to going outside for twenty minutes as well? The two don't have to overlap—you could meditate outside, or watch the sunrise instead of something active—but you could certainly combine them. They have similar benefits, essentially building a "reset" button into the day. Exercise is a known mood booster; fresh air is too. Combining the two can result in feeling like you're on top of the world, even on a normal Tuesday.

A few strategic choices can make this habit more doable:

1. Get good gear.

As the saying goes, there's no bad weather, only bad clothing. A good raincoat, rain pants, and waterproof boots make a downpour a minor inconvenience. Chemical hand warmers tucked in gloves can make even those of us with poor circulation feel toasty. A long, insulated coat that covers your upper legs will make cold weather more tolerable than one that stops at your waist, and anything below about 15 degrees requires a face covering.

2. Experiment with time of day.

If heat is more your challenge, there's a limit to how many layers you can remove. So instead, play around with "when." Noon might be brutal, but a sunrise cup of coffee on the porch can be a communion with astonishment. Same with a night walk to look at the moon.

3. Know what you'll do if the weather (or your schedule) changes.

Even if you have good gear, you might not have the right gear for the occasion. Plus, life seldom goes as planned. If you truly want to make something a daily habit, figure out a second choice for those days when your first choice isn't available. If it's raining and you don't have an umbrella, maybe you can take the kids for a walk in the evening when the weather clears. Amy has found a sheltered spot of trees where she walks on the days when gale-force winds thwart her original route. If an emergency trip to the dentist derails your afternoon, maybe you can sit outside at night, listening to the crickets, after the kids go to bed. Creating a back-up plan for anything important (see Rule 5) vastly increases the chances that it happens.

Once you decide to go outside for twenty minutes a day, you can tap into much more wonder by simply being open to new experiences. As we'll explore in later chapters, memories last far longer than any immediate anxiousness or discomfort—within reason. Amy doesn't recommend running marathons in sub-zero temperatures. But short of that, you might be surprised at what you can do.

On one Monday night, Amy had planned to bring her two boys to a weekly community walk/run through Palmer. The weather was fine at the Bushatz house. Palmer, three miles away, appeared to have been hit by a monsoon. "The streets were flooded," she says. "There were pictures that evening of someone kayaking through the street as a joke."

The situation was ridiculous. They hadn't brought rain gear but it wouldn't have helped if they had—the water was higher than their boots. And yet ten people still showed up to run. So as a group, they decided to see what would happen. "We ran through knee-high puddles," Amy says. They laughed and splashed and had this otherwise normal Monday seared happily into their brains. "We were basically swimming through this run. It was a fantastic, memorable rain run that I now look back on, and I'm so glad we didn't turn around and go home," she says. "It was some of the most fun we've ever had."

Your turn

◆

MOVE BY 3 P.M.

Planning questions:

1. On average, how much exercise do you currently get per week? When do you usually do this?

2. What kind of exercise do you do?

3. What sort of physical activity could you do for ten minutes before 3 p.m. during an average day? If you're already exercising early most days, consider how you could add ten or fifteen minutes of movement midday.

4. Think about today: When could you do this activity today? (If it's already past 3 p.m., consider when you could exercise before 3 p.m. on a day like today.)

5. How about tomorrow? When could you do this activity tomorrow?

6. What challenges might keep you from building more physical activity into your life?

7. How can you address these challenges?

Implementation questions:

1. About how much exercise did you get this week? When did you do this? What did you do?

2. What effects did you see in your life from moving by 3 p.m. most days?

3. What challenges did you face in implementing this week's strategy?

4. How did you deal with these challenges?

5. If you needed to modify this rule, how did you do so?

6. How likely are you to continue using this rule in your life?

PART 2

◆

Make Good Things Happen

Habits for doing more of what matters

*D*aily life can feature maddening inefficiencies. The jam-up around a double-parked car adds fifteen minutes to a trip. A recurring meeting—that has long outlived its utility—drags on as someone digresses into complaints about an unrelated project.

As we watch these minutes slip away like sand in an hourglass, we come to the logical conclusion that time must be scarce. We hope to claw some of it back. That's why time-management literature tends to focus on how to shave time off the everyday activities that we have at least some control over. Add this time up, and people can finally make space for the pleasures that seemed elusive before.

I will admit that I read a lot of this material. I'm always hoping I'll learn some amazing life hack. I'll find hours in the day I didn't know existed. Then, inevitably, the tips turn out to be something like "clean the shower while you're in it" or the seemingly clever idea that if you send a lot of emails where the answer is "OK," you could just type "K" instead of "OK."

If only that were the secret to a good life, right?

Sadly, nothing much will change on this unpredictable planet, or even in your own life, by skipping a letter or two in your emails, no matter how many emails you send. You will not suddenly create close connections with family and friends, or make progress on your professional and personal priorities, or experience the sorts of weekends that leave you feeling warm and happy on Monday morning.

If you wish to enjoy these things, then the wiser course is to approach time from the other direction. First, you fill your life with what matters to you. Then, you will naturally spend less time on shower cleaning or email or whatever else seems to fill the hours.

The first section of Tranquility by Tuesday focused on how to calm the chaos by building habits that support well-being. In time, these habits also help us become strategic about our days, our weeks, and our hours. With these rules in place, life feels a lot more doable.

This second section builds on that foundation by showing

how to make good things happen. After thinking about what we'd like to expand in our lives, we create a workable plan for when we can do these things. We build resilient schedules that allow for life's complexities. We find ways to make each week more memorable, and we find space for a joyful commitment apart from work and family obligations.

Taken together, these rules will make life feel less like a slog. Each week becomes something to look forward to. We also develop the serenity that comes from knowing we will make progress on our goals even when life doesn't go as planned. We have the power to build the lives we want. These next four chapters show how.

RULE 4

Three Times a Week Is a Habit

Things don't have to happen daily—nor do they have to happen at the same time every day—in order to count in our lives.

*L*eah Burman had figured out a good rhythm for life with little kids. This Maryland-based software developer and Agile coach used to exercise around 5:30 a.m. most mornings before work. She and her husband Ian, a collegiate athletic coach, would spend time together in the ninety-minute slot after the kids went to bed (8:30 p.m.) and before Leah did (10 p.m.).

Then the children got older, as children do. Suddenly, this schedule no longer worked. The preteen Burman children stayed up as late as their parents. They didn't really need a babysitter anymore, but because they did need some supervision, and had activities, Leah and Ian flexed their work schedules to accommodate the school hours. Leah would begin work at 6 a.m., with Ian covering the morning kid shift. Then Leah would handle the after-school time, while Ian was at practice.

Net result: They no longer had any time without the kids on weekday evenings. Also, the 6 a.m. work start "has killed my morning workout routine," Leah told me when we first corresponded in late 2019 about her schedule. "I've tried to motivate myself to work out while the kids are at afternoon activities or later at night, and it just doesn't work well for me." The result: "I end up skipping a majority of the time."

Leah wasn't exactly happy with this state of affairs. She wanted to figure out new options for exercise and couple time in the middle of her full life. So I asked her to keep track of her time for a week to see what we could do.

The first week she tracked was . . . impressive. This is a hazard of offering to do time makeovers for people who already read productivity blogs and books. Leah was using her commute to listen to podcasts. She had planned all sorts of weekend adventures, a habit she told me she developed when the kids were little and she was solo-parenting twenty-some weekends of the year while her husband's team was competing. The Burman family went boating with friends. They went to a county fair, apple picking, and to a vineyard for a wine tasting too. Leah had carved out work time for "deep work," as productivity expert Cal Newport calls these focused sessions, and labeled it as such on her log. This was already expert-level schedule awareness.

As for exercise and couple time—the source of her vexation—this was honestly not so bad. She had negotiated to work from home one day a week (this was in 2019, before much of the world adopted the practice), and she and Ian had lunch on that day before he headed out to coach afternoon sessions. She lifted weights on Saturday, and went for an evening walk with friends in the middle of the week.

In both cases, it wasn't a lot, but it was *something*. This turns out to be a life-altering realization. Perhaps that sounds dramatic, but in this chapter, I'm going to argue the case. There is a big distinction between "never" and "not as much as I want." The latter invites incremental changes that can, over time, change a schedule. Changing a schedule can, in fact, change our entire attitude toward life.

So as Leah looked for space to lift weights and have couple time, I shared **Tranquility by Tuesday Rule 4: Three times a week is a habit**.

Aiming to do something daily—as in seven days a week, or even five—can be challenging. Certain healthy habits, such as moving for ten minutes (see Rule 3) or brushing your teeth, are worth the bother. But for many things, daily isn't necessary. Things do not have to happen daily, nor do they have to happen at the same time every day, in order to count in our lives. I maintain that anything that happens three times a week counts as happening regularly.

That's good news, because aiming for three times a week can be quite doable. Many times, when people observe their schedules, they discover that they are already doing something once or even twice a week. Getting to three requires tweaks, not a total lifestyle overhaul. Good things are already happening. All you have to do is add a few more good things. Success—that is, making time for what matters to you—is within reach. And when success is within reach, people make success happen. This is as much a mindset shift as an actual schedule change, but mindset shifts are powerful. They can change our entire relationship with time.

In Leah's case, she didn't need to wake up at 4 a.m. Monday through Friday in order to fit in weightlifting. She could do her routine on both Saturday and Sunday mornings at a far more reasonable time when the house was still quiet. She could also lift weights in her basement on her work-from-home day, consciously subbing that time for her commute. That would be three times right there—and would meet the definition of a habit. With just a small change, she would be the sort of person who had a regular strength-training routine.

As for couple time, the Burmans just needed to think beyond Saturday night (complicated with Ian's team travel schedule) or the weekday post–8:30 p.m. slot that had worked before. The weekly lunch at home was a nice idea. Leah mentioned that in the past they had sometimes done a during-the-week date night at a neighborhood place. She mused that the two of them could go out for a post-family-dinner drink some evening that worked, and leave their older child in charge. They would be back in about an hour, not having missed much. She noted that they also had a porch off their bedroom, which could provide some privacy from the kids if they availed themselves of it. They could aim to spend a few minutes there on weekends—which would get them to three times a week of conscious connection.

Leah decided to try these strategies. She came back to me a few weeks later with another time log that was even more impressive than the first. She had lifted weights three times, just as she planned. As she told me, in her mind exercise was something she did when she had childcare or her husband was covering. But this wasn't exactly necessary with older kids, and so she needed to "throw away older conceptions about time"—something all of us should consider on our journey to tranquility. In Leah's case, her almost-teenagers slept long enough on weekend mornings that she could probably have run a marathon before they wanted to get up. She and Ian had lunch, went out for drinks, and had several long porch conversations (not just one!). She noted that they were "happily surprised to find how much time we could unearth if we were intentional about it."

When I followed up with her in 2021, she noted that she was continuing with these new habits. During the COVID lockdowns, she and Ian began ordering an appetizer board and cocktails from a local company that would deliver the treats every Friday afternoon. The kids would entertain themselves and the two of them would welcome the weekend by sitting on the porch together. "It's striking to me that the changes we made from your time makeover have remained in place, even with a pandemic," she reported. And yes, she was still lifting weights on weekends.

She scheduled her weightlifting sessions for Friday, Saturday, Sunday, and Tuesday (with four scheduled, at least three would happen, a concept we'll return to in the next chapter). Between that and the daily walking (moving by 3 p.m.!), she was exercising a lot. The "three times a week is a habit" rule had "made a great difference in my life and stood the test of time," she noted.

Escaping the twenty-four-hour trap

We all have activities we'd like to devote more time to: hobbies, spiritual practices, playing musical instruments, creative work, eating family meals. We know these activities would boost our spirits, yet people get discouraged because life gets busy. We wind up doing these things we wish to do frequently only once or twice a week.

Unfortunately, once or twice a week can feel minimal, because the default mindset is to view our lives in days. If you do something once a week, then six out of seven days you didn't do it. Most nights you go to bed feeling like you didn't achieve your goals. You discount what you have done and can easily feel defeated.

But there's no reason we have to fall into this twenty-four-hour trap. With the "three times a week is a habit" mindset, we start to look at time more holistically, and at our lives more compassionately. We give ourselves credit for what we are doing, and we look for little ways to scale up, without the pressure of aiming for daily. "Three times a week is a habit" gives us a doable goal for developing a desired identity.

For instance, maybe you want to eat regular family meals. With kid activities and parent work schedules, no one is unveiling a steaming pot roast, Norman Rockwell–style, at 6 p.m. Monday through Friday. But then you observe your life for a while and you see that your family is generally eating dinner together on Sundays. You already have one stamp on your card. Now all you need to do is find a few more regular meal times during the week—maybe a new Tuesday morning breakfast tradition, and Friday pizza night?—and just like that, you are a family that eats together.

Or maybe you have visions of reading chapter books aloud with your brood. Bedtime is often chaotic, though, or you work late or travel early in the week. But maybe you see that Thursday and Friday nights are generally available. This happy realization sends you hunting for other literary spots. Maybe you could read a chapter over breakfast on Saturday mornings. Now you're making it through three chapters a week, and a book a month. You are a person who reads lengthy books with your kids. You can adopt this hoped-for identity, even with everything else you've got going on.

If you want to make time for something that matters to you, stop looking for the perfect time every single day. Very few people do anything at the exact same time every single day. Even people who claim to have "daily" routines often don't. They do their "daily" routine Monday through Friday, which is only five days a week. Look a little closer and you find that, often, Friday doesn't make it into the "routine" category. That puts us at four times a week. If the person skips holidays, or vacations, or sick days, the average over the long haul is probably a lot closer to three days a week than seven. I find it interesting that people who generally do things Monday, Tuesday, Wednesday, and Thursday often consider that to be a "daily" habit, whereas people who do things Friday, Saturday, and Sunday do not. I'm not sure where this sense comes from that weekdays count but weekends do not, but there's nothing inherently more virtuous about one combination of days than another.

In any case, perfect does not need to be the enemy of good. This is the most obvious reason I teach this rule.

But the deeper idea is just as important. The twenty-four-hour trap is responsible for many of the false-choice narratives that limit people's lives. Thinking "three times a week is a habit," and remembering that a week has 168 hours to play with, is a simple shift that changes our mindset from scarcity to abundance.

For instance, if a week has 168 hours, then you quickly see that "full-time" work doesn't take anywhere close to the full quantity of your time. If you work 40 hours a week, and sleep eight hours a night (56 per week) you have 72 hours for other things. This is almost twice as much time as you are working. The usual narrative that pits full-time work against family, or physical health, or community involvement, must now argue that it is impossible, in 72 hours, to find time for family adventures, plus a few thirty-minute slots for exercise, and to volunteer for two to three hours as well. From studying people's time logs, I'd wager that you can find time for these things in 62 hours (working 50 hours a week) or even 52 hours (working 60 hours a week—which is about the maximum sustained average that time logs show, even for people in intense jobs).

With the 168-hour mindset, weekends move from an afterthought to an important chunk of the week. I track my time on weekly spreadsheets that begin on Monday at 5 a.m. If the week starts on Monday at 5 a.m., the midway point of the week turns out to be 5 p.m. on *Thursday*. While 5 p.m. on Thursday may feel like the *end* of the week, there is just as much time after this midpoint as there is before. (And yes, I understand that more of this second half of the week is spent sleeping. But when you run the numbers with this in mind, the halfway point for waking hours turns out to be early afternoon Thursday. It is nowhere near Wednesday, which people often consider to be the middle of the week).

A week is not an infinite amount of time, of course. But it is a lot of time. When we remember that three times a week is a habit, we approach our 168 hours with a sense of possibility. If we wish to add something meaningful to our lives, the time is probably there. Like Leah, we might be surprised at how much time we can unearth. We just need to change things up a little bit to make what matters happen.

Participant perspectives:
Ideas for implementation

After introducing Rule 4, I asked the Tranquility by Tuesday participants to brainstorm various activities they would like to do more frequently. Then I asked them to choose one specific activity that they would like to focus on during the project. Ideally this was something they did occasionally, and wanted to do more often.

People came up with lots of different ideas. The most popular answer was to read, though this usually meant a specific sort of reading, such as reading professional development books or religious texts. Several people wanted to write or journal. Others wanted to do arts and crafts. Like Leah, a number of people who were walking for ten minutes daily, thanks to Rule 3, wanted to do full formal workouts. People wanted time with their partners, or one-on-one time with children. Others mentioned cooking family meals, practicing new languages, or playing musical instruments. One person wanted to research a child's medical condition. Another wanted to do three sessions a week tackling bigger house projects.

The majority of people (57 percent) had done their chosen activity at least once within the past week, while another 23 percent had done the activity within the past few weeks. People were doing these things occasionally. They just weren't doing them as often as they wanted.

I asked people to think about the upcoming week, and to think about when they could aim to do their chosen activity. I asked them to list at least three times. I asked them to think about any challenges they might face in doing the activity during those three times, and how they might address these challenges.

This exercise had people thinking about their schedules and thinking through logistics. For instance, one person who wanted to do a Bible study decided to "make a sign in my office to remember that I'll do Bible study at 1:30 p.m. on Monday, Tuesday, and Friday." One person who wanted to practice the piano mentioned finding times when other people wouldn't be watching TV in the same room. (I noted that this person could also tell other family members that they needed to stop watching TV!)

People added items to their daily to-do lists on the chosen days, or put three checkboxes on a weekly planner page. One person looking to build a yoga practice pledged to "pick out the videos I want to do in advance and put a reminder in my phone for the specific time." Some people who were moving by 3 p.m. during one work break elected to use a different work break for the week's chosen activity. A few people chose three mornings per week for exercise; others with intense work schedules identified spots on Friday and the two weekend days.

Participant perspectives: Identifying obstacles

People identified plenty of challenges that might keep them from doing their chosen activities three times per week. There were the usual suspects, such as work crises. One person rued that during this particular week, "I left late every day. I cannot plan anything at the very end of the workday, apparently." Then there's the fact that it's easier to scroll through Twitter than to create something, as one potential artist noted.

Some challenges were practical. If you want to paint three times a week, you need your paints to be accessible. You're probably not going to practice the drums while the baby is asleep (unless they're electronic drums and you're using headphones). People who wanted to connect with their partners needed their partners to be available for such connection, which introduced another layer of schedule complexity. People who wanted to do things that required childcare needed support from their partners or other caregivers, and even folks with older kids noted that it "feels hard to slip away to a quiet space when the rest of the family is home," as one person put it.

Some folks just forgot. Life gets busy and a week later you get another email from Laura and you remember that you never got around to your woodworking projects.

These practical challenges were generally surmountable with a little planning. People began keeping their embroidery work close to them, so it was available, and put those weights in their home office. They studied their gym schedules and found classes that met at more convenient times.

More intriguing to me was that, for some people, this rule surfaced some deeper issues. Two in particular stood out as most common.

1. Avoidance.

A few folks holding on to the it-must-be-daily narrative realized they were struggling with perfectionism or imposter syndrome—"It's been too long, it's so embarrassing!" as one person wrote of attempting creative efforts.

Sometimes it feels safer to go with "never." If you can't do something at the same time every single day, which you probably can't as a person with a full-time job and family responsibilities, then you can't do it at all, and—most important here—*it's not your fault that you aren't doing it.* Hence, you don't need to take the risks that come along with making different choices. You can lament the perfect paintings in your head that you don't have time to create, rather than creating less-than-perfect paintings during your three weekly painting sessions.

2. Guilt.

Then there was the "I don't deserve to have fun" issue. Some people struggle with the idea of actively choosing to do anything that is separate from immediate work or family concerns, an issue that resurfaced with one of the later rules ("Take one night for you") and explains why a handful of Tranquility by Tuesday participants chose chores such as laundry as their three-times-a-week-is-a-habit activity.

These issues came up a lot. One woman wrote, "I feel like I can't do this sort of work [creative writing] while I'm 'on the clock,'"—that is, during time she could be working or handling family responsibilities. "I don't feel like I deserve to dedicate time to a pet project that is solely for my own pleasure, not to make money." Some participants spoke of the pressure to use childcare hours for work or other necessities only, not for personal pursuits, with a number of people including their partners in this "childcare" category. In other words, it's OK to ask your partner to cover for an hour so you can go to the hardware store. It is not OK to ask for an hour on the weekend to practice the flute. This belief meant that the time available for personal pursuits was time with children, unless they were sleeping, which limited the options.

Sometimes these narratives require extensive work to unravel. Perhaps this rule can be a nudge to start doing that work.

If you do find yourself in possession of these beliefs, though, I'd argue that this rule's sheer practicality can help change your perspective.

If you feel guilty for "wasting time" on a chosen activity that is just for you, and particularly an activity that you're not going to do well at first, you're going to waste time for only three short sessions a week. That's it. Three twenty-minute sessions is a mere one hour out of the 168 hours in a week. I've never met anyone who doesn't waste at least sixty minutes over seven days.

On the flip side, if you feel guilty for *not* doing your chosen activity more, thinking "three times a week is a habit" can be liberating as well. If you've chosen three specific times in a week to do what you'd like to do, then you are maintaining the habit while freeing yourself up, mentally, during every other minute of your time. You don't feel bad about watching TV instead of hauling out the paint set on Saturday afternoon if Saturday afternoon isn't one of your three slots. Just like that, guilt-free downtime is achieved.

The results

Most people pushed through the challenges. After a week, 62 percent of people indicated on the survey that they had spent more time on their chosen activity. The median reported additional time was sixty minutes. Maybe this doesn't sound like much, but in busy lives where every minute feels spoken for, finding an extra hour to practice the piano, lift weights, or read for professional development can make life feel very different. People were surprised at how doable their desires suddenly seemed:

- "By setting the goal of crafting/knitting three times per week, I actually remembered to do it."
- "I believe in the importance of a daily prayer time but have not always been successful in finding a time to do it consistently. By making it a priority and putting it on

my calendar for three times this week I was able to get
it done."

As people repeated this mantra that "three times a week is a
habit," they saw a few major benefits.

First, several noted that this small change shifted their time
narratives—that is, the stories we all tell ourselves about where
the time is going and what people like us should be doing. "I
identified times that I could fit [my chosen activity] in rather
than assuming I just didn't have time," one person wrote, with
another noting that this rule made her "conscious of the agency
I have over my schedule."

Newly enamored with this agency, some people went all in.
While the median additional time spent on a chosen activity was
sixty minutes, the range went up to fifteen hours. People launched
or rebooted all sorts of projects. For instance, the woman who
wrote of feeling guilty doing creative writing while "on the clock"
realized that three times a week was doable—she was often doing a little something almost that often anyway—and was also a
great frequency for blogging.

"I decided writing was a habit for me. I *was* a writer—just the
validation I needed. My goal was to have [my website] up and
running by my thirty-fourth birthday (today), and I've managed
just that. I'm so grateful that I finally found the courage to give
myself permission to prioritize this dream."

She wasn't the only newly prolific writer. Another person
who started writing three times a week realized the truth that

devoting regular blocks of time to creative work makes you come up with more ideas: "I found myself thinking about what I was going to write when I sat down to do it. The wheels are turning in my brain again."

Since people generally chose enjoyable activities (at least those who didn't select chores!), it's not surprising that, as a second major benefit, people reported that they were having a lot of fun. A person who committed to journaling three times a week wrote that "I looked forward to the time block I set aside for this, and had fun doing the activity itself. It is also something tangible I can look back on . . . Plus it was relaxing."

Beyond the sheer pleasure of doing chosen activities more frequently, people liked this rule's focus on making success doable. Three times is a very specific number—helpful for those who in the past had just wanted to do an activity "more"—and it is also achievable in a busy life. Many participants confessed to "all or nothing" thinking that had diminished the pleasure of their chosen activities in the past.

"I felt like I was actually choosing to do the thing that feels life-giving to me, rather than lamenting the fact that I'm not doing it," one person wrote.

This framing—that it is OK to do a little something, or just do it adequately rather than perfectly—by itself turned disappointment into satisfaction for people who spoke of ditching the guilt:

◆ "In January, I completed a thirty-day yoga challenge, and actually did yoga every day. In February, I kept up with the practice, but didn't manage to do it every day, which made me feel like I had somehow 'failed' at yoga. By setting a goal of yoga three or four times a week, I reframed my idea of success."

◆ "Having a goal of cooking three times and reaching it made me proud of myself, especially because it was an intense workweek for me. If I hadn't set this goal, I would have felt bad for 'never cooking' and relying on my husband and take-out. It took away the guilt."

Removing the guilt is no small thing. Indeed, several people reported that because they weren't trying to do the activity daily, "the pressure was off," as one person put it, "so I actually did the activity more often." Some people even wound up doing their chosen activity all seven days during Week 4 of the Tranquility by Tuesday project, enjoying the sense that this frequency was a bonus, rather than a bare minimum requirement. "I know I can 'fall back' on three times a week when work gets crazy again," one person wrote.

Success is possible, even in a complicated life

The essence of tranquility is feeling serene, and it is hard to feel serene when you feel like a failure, especially when you feel like a failure at something that's supposed to *help* with tranquility, like yoga. When you feel like you are doing the things that matter to you, and doing them frequently enough that they matter, then you can feel satisfied with your schedule. This happy change in mindset is likely the reason that desire to continue with this rule was high (5.99 on my 7-point scale).

If you take nothing else from this book, I hope you remember this: Success is possible, even in the midst of a complex and occasionally chaotic life. You do not need to wait for some less-hectic future time to become the person you want to be. With a different perspective, and a focus on doing what you can, you can be that person *now*.

Certainly that is the lesson some Tranquility by Tuesday participants learned.

One woman wrote that "As a forty-something mom of a four-year-old, one of my biggest struggles is the feeling of dissatisfaction that I have sometimes about not getting to do the things I want to do with regularity." Her later-in-life transition to parenthood "has been so wonderful in many ways, but it has also been a profound identity shift for me solely because it has made me feel less in control of my own time."

Any parent can sympathize. But we can also take comfort from this realization: "Just this one idea—if I do something three times a week it is a habit—has really made me remember that, yes, I am still a person who reads! Who pursues fitness! Who makes home-cooked meals! Who spends meaningful time with my husband!" She might not have been doing those things as often as she used to, or as spontaneously as she could when she had fewer responsibilities. "But if I am finding three times a week to do something, it is a habit or a hobby or a PART OF MY IDENTITY."

I love seeing all-caps answers on survey forms. It is a good indication that, as this respondent put it, a rule has been life-changing—and a simpler shift than she thought possible.

I'm guessing that you too may be walking around with faulty time narratives of how often things have to happen, or what is possible in your life. The "Three times a week is a habit" rule can help shift all of these. How would you like to describe yourself? "I am the kind of person who . . ." Whatever this is, could you do this three times a week? Perhaps not, but often the answer is yes. As we aim to build lives with space for what matters, that is really all it takes.

Take the next step

◆

DESIGN YOUR IDEAL WEEK

To figure out when you will do something three times a week, you need a good sense of your schedule. The best way to gain that sense is to actually keep track of your time.

Thousands of people have participated in my time-tracking challenges over the years. The process can be enlightening. If you haven't logged your time before, get a spreadsheet, get a notebook, or get an app and try it out. You write down what you're doing, as often as you remember, in as much detail as you think will be helpful. The goal is to keep going for a full 168 hours. My guess is that you'll learn a lot about your life. You'll learn a lot about your values, and how your choices play out in life's daily rhythms. Even just trying to reconstruct what you've done with your time is eye-opening (wrote one person: "Half-hour time slots with absolutely no recollection—was I abducted?").

But let's say you've done that. Then what?

My friend Matt Altmix, co-host, with Joel Larsgaard, of the "How to Money" podcast, tracked his time for over a year. It was a familiar process; he's tracked his spending for years as well. Then he realized an additional parallel. With money, "Tracking spending is an important step, but it's not the same as creating a budget," Matt told me. You don't just want to know where your money has gone. You want to figure out, ideally, where it should go in the future—based on your obligations and desires. "That's what I needed to do with my time," he says.

So Matt decided to create a time budget, which he began calling "Matt's Perfect Week." Given his work and family obligations, what would an ideal week look like?

He got a blank calendar and figured out the big categories. Then he pondered where everything he wanted to do could go. He built in exercise time. He figured out that evenings with his four young kids would likely go better if he stopped working at 4:30 p.m., rather than 5 or 5:30 p.m., so that gave him a nudge to investigate some efficiencies. He built in time when he and his wife Kate could alternate spending one-on-one time with the kids. He saw that after the kids went down, and he and Kate did their chores and debriefed, he had two solid hours to do whatever he wanted.

Seeing this available chunk of time made him far more motivated to not just piddle this time away. He began instituting "social Tuesdays"—he could visit someone's porch after kid bedtime if Kate could cover, or a friend could visit him. He realized that he could watch a two-hour movie and still get to bed on time, something that, before building the time budget, would have seemed irresponsible.

Not every week hits the ideal. Indeed, no week does exactly. But knowing the contours of "Matt's Perfect Week" makes Matt a lot more likely to attempt to make the ideal a reality.

I'm guessing you'll find the same thing as well. So after you've tracked your time, try creating your own realistic ideal week—one that acknowledges your responsibilities, but shows you at your best. Pull out a blank calendar (I'd suggest a spreadsheet with all 168 hours of the week). Put in what you'd like your week to look like. Ask yourself:

1. When would you wake up on various days?
2. What would you do in the mornings?
3. When would you work?
4. What would you like your workdays to look like?
5. How about your weekday evenings?
6. What would you do during a realistic, ideal weekend?

Yes, your time will vary a lot, but you could create a general template. On a good weekend, for instance, I'd do at least one long run somewhere scenic, plan a half-day family adventure, sing on Sunday morning with my choir, and enjoy some sort of adult-only fun.

When we get frustrated with life, we often think that we need to make big changes. What I love about designing an ideal week is that it shows how small changes can have a big impact.

Maybe you have noticed over the years that you get a lot done in the late afternoons going into the early evenings. But because you also value eating as a family, you've assumed that you just have to sacrifice this work time when you might achieve a state of flow. Then you decide to design your ideal week. You plot out your ideal work hours, and dinner time, and you see that maybe, just maybe, someone *else* could be responsible for cooking dinner three times per week, or if nothing else, your eating could move a little later. Now you can seize more of your productive hours and enjoy family dinners too. Or maybe you see that by waking up thirty minutes earlier on two weekday mornings, and then using a few lunch breaks, you can make space for exercise *and* creative writing, each multiple times per week. You don't have to pit one against the other.

Life won't always work as anyone wishes. That's the reason for the next chapter, which talks about creating a resilient schedule. An ideal schedule will also have to change over time as life changes. But if you know the ideal schedule, at least for now, then you can make decisions with that schedule in mind. As your experienced time gets closer to your ideal time, you'll be happier. That's a great thing to experience—as many times per week as possible.

Your turn

◆

THREE TIMES A WEEK IS A HABIT

Planning questions:

1. List some activities you'd like to do more frequently in your life.

2. Choose one specific activity to focus on for the next week.

3. When did you last do this activity?

4. Looking forward to the next week, when could this happen? List at least three times.

5. What obstacles might prevent you from doing this activity three times a week?

6. How can you address these challenges?

Implementation questions:

1. What activity did you choose to focus on three times this week?

2. Did you spend more time on your chosen activity this week than in previous weeks?

3. If so, how much more time did you spend on it?

4. What was the impact of aiming to do this activity three times per week?

5. What challenges, if any, affected your ability to do this activity three times this week?

6. How did you address these challenges?

7. Did you need to modify this rule to work for you? How?

8. How likely are you to continue using this rule in your life?

RULE 5

Create a Back-up Slot

Anyone can make a perfect schedule. Time-management masters make resilient schedules.

Many professions have their hoops. Accountants and lawyers work to make partner in their firms. Academics pursue "tenure"—officially a designation that your position is permanent, but more celebrated as a mark of success than anything else. To achieve this distinction, professors generally need to do a certain volume of original research. Then they need to get their results published in peer-reviewed journals.

Elizabeth Morphis, a professor in the education department at SUNY Old Westbury, was headed into the tenure window a few years ago when she sought out my time-management advice. She needed to create space to write up her research and submit her articles for publication, and she needed to do this amid everything else she had going on in her life.

This was easier said than done. Elizabeth, her husband, and their two young girls had moved to the north shore of Long Island for her job. This was convenient for her, but meant that her husband was commuting more than an hour into New York City for his job. Since she was the one physically there, Elizabeth wound up being the default parent during the week if kids got sick or after-school sitters canceled. As an education professor, Elizabeth's core job responsibilities involved supervising dozens of inexperienced teachers as they practiced their new skills in the classroom. Needless to say, much could go wrong there too.

As a result, her time logs showed her making space for all manner of other people's needs. This was all noble and good, but it was not her research and writing.

So I asked Elizabeth to look at her schedule and propose a few time blocks she could devote to these things. Since I had told her about my rule that "three times a week is a habit," she came up with three slots beyond her basic work hours when she could reliably take on these extra tasks: 6 to 7:30 a.m. on Mondays and Fridays before her husband left for the train, and 5:45 to 6:45 p.m. on Wednesday nights when she had childcare coverage for the night class she taught.

In a perfect week that might have been fine, but you don't need to be a professor to deduce how easily those three small spots could disappear. What if Elizabeth overslept? What if her husband occasionally needed to leave for work early? What if the babysitter was late, or a student asked to meet right before class? Pretty soon she'd be down to just an hour or two each week, which is hardly enough for what she really did consider a top professional priority.

So we went back to the schedule and found some longer blocks. Since Elizabeth was managing much of the after-school shift during the week, we decided that she could take one day off from this. She didn't teach on Thursday afternoons, so if she arranged for their usual sitter to pick the girls up at school, then from about lunch time on she could devote a four-to-five-hour shift to research and writing. Elizabeth's husband was also an underused resource. Given that she did the lion's share of the during-the-week parenting, she knew that he was willing to do more on the weekends. They agreed that Saturday afternoons would generally be Daddy time. Elizabeth would work from 12 to 4 p.m. or so on her projects.

That already seemed like a lot of time, but then we added one final tweak: If for some reason Saturday afternoon didn't work, she'd do this window on Sunday.

With two long sessions scheduled per week, and an official back-up slot, the odds were good that she would get at least one four-hour stretch for focused, tenure-seeking work, no matter what came up.

Elizabeth agreed to try this schedule. Sure enough, during the first week, the babysitter got sick on Thursday. Elizabeth's tenure-seeking work slot got chopped into little bits.

In much literature on work and life, this would be the moment where we lament the impossibility of having it all. But Elizabeth had no need for this lament. Because the weekend slots were still available, she scored several hours that week to work on her projects. Then the next week she got both Thursday and a weekend slot, which made more progress possible.

As she became more assured of getting at least one long chunk of writing time each week, a funny thing started to happen. She began planning specific research and writing tasks for each week to eliminate writing anxiety and to help her allocate time efficiently. For instance, she took a colleague up on an offer to read a paper she was working on for a revise and resubmit. She sent the colleague what she'd done after her Thursday session, and got it back in time to incorporate the feedback during her weekend session.

With these big blocks of time—and back-up slots—in place, Elizabeth's pace of article submission increased rapidly. Then, of course, COVID hit. This created all kinds of complications for both teaching and teaching people how to teach when schools no longer met in person. However, when I got back in touch with Elizabeth in 2021 as things were settling down, she shared that she had continued to use the back-up-slot strategy to ensure she had space for career-advancing work. Indeed, this strategy had allowed her to keep moving forward in a situation where I suspect 99 percent of people would have figured, "OK life, *you got me.*"

At some point in March of 2021 she found a call for journal submissions with a deadline of late March. She had the data for a project she wanted to publish, so she made a plan to finish the article the weekend before the Friday submission deadline. "I had planned to work all Saturday that weekend, hoping that I'd finish and just have minor edits to do the following week," she says. But she decided to plan some back-up slots during the week "just in case I didn't get as much finished over the weekend."

Then Friday night arrived. Her husband felt sick—a normal sort of thing at first, which then got worse. Eventually, she took him to the emergency room with what turned out to be severe food poisoning. The staff there told her to come back to get him around 3 a.m. But he wasn't released until midday Saturday, which meant that neither Saturday (when she was going back and forth to the hospital) nor Sunday (when she was helping him recuperate) was exactly amenable to article writing.

Having your spouse in the hospital is a valid reason for missing a deadline. There would be other calls for articles. Elizabeth knew this, but she also knew that she had all those back-up slots. Once she had assured herself that her husband was going to be all right, she realized that missing the deadline wasn't actually a foregone conclusion. "Because I had scheduled that extra time the following week, I was surprisingly calm," she says. In this state of tranquility, she made a list of what she needed to do. When the kids were in school on Monday, she used the back-up slot she had built in. She was able to finalize the article during her Thursday slot and submit it—one day ahead of schedule.

That is the power of **Tranquility by Tuesday Rule 5: Create**

a back-up slot. As Elizabeth discovered, anything that you truly want to have happen needs the equivalent of a "rain date"—which is an incredibly useful concept, if you think about it. When organizers for an outdoor event schedule a "rain date," they are acknowledging that much can go predictably wrong; it is right there in the "rain date" name. There is no question about whether things will be rescheduled, or when. They will be—on the official rain date. People know not to put anything unmovable in the back-up slot. Most likely the slot won't be needed, but its existence vastly increases the chances of the original event happening, even if not when originally planned.

As I've studied people's schedules, and their goals, I've realized that we need a lot more rain dates in life. We can hope to make space for the "important but not urgent" things that would enrich our lives. We can schedule time to go to the gym, practice the alto sax, or write blog posts. But when life is busy, this time can be taken away from us, whether that's due to work crises, illnesses, or just a kid waking up early and resisting all attempts to lure him back to bed.

It is easy to get frustrated about these things. They are indeed frustrating. But I find it helps to remember this: Anyone can make a perfect schedule. True time-management masters make resilient schedules. They harbor no illusions that life will be easy, and so they shape their hours to foster progress even when things don't go as planned. In doing so, they make life feel a lot more tranquil, even when it is hard.

How to build a resilient schedule

Creating a back-up slot for the things that matter starts with figuring out what matters. I asked Tranquility by Tuesday participants to think about things that were important to them but had a tendency to get bumped from the schedule. Maybe it's a Saturday-morning long run with a friend that keeps getting canceled because of rain or complicated family schedules. If the original time doesn't work, when else can you go? You might plan to research a new client on Tuesday afternoon, but if a meeting runs over, when else can you tackle this priority? Or perhaps you carved out time to work on your business plan on Thursday, but your toddler was up multiple times in the night and you are having trouble concentrating. You can still do a little something—something is always better than nothing—but you'll feel more calm about feeling unproductive if you know your partner has agreed to take the toddler on Saturday morning if you need extra time.

Just as an outdoor graduation ceremony needs its own specific rain date, the most important activities in your life need specific back-up slots.

That said, creating specific back-up slots can get unwieldy as the priorities stack up. We also don't always know, during Friday planning, everything we'll need to do by the end of the next week. So here's a practical shortcut for this rule: **Get in the habit of leaving regularly scheduled open space in your schedule**.

That way you have a back-up slot for whatever priority you need to move.

This open space can take different forms for different people. Maybe it's an hour every afternoon, or maybe it's one morning a week. Some people who schedule things on the hour in the morning might schedule on the half-hour in the afternoon, to force at least thirty minutes of open space (though I'd recommend aiming for ninety minutes of open space so you have time to think: Book your last morning appointment at 11 a.m. and your first afternoon appointment at 1:30 p.m.). When the morning's appointments run over, as they inevitably will, the afternoon appointments won't then also fall over like dominoes.

My personal approach to this rule is to keep Fridays open. I find this doable if I "plan tight, then plan light"—a mantra that many Tranquility by Tuesday participants reported finding helpful. This means designating times on Monday and Tuesday for all of the week's high-priority tasks. The minutes at the beginning of the week will feel a little full, but this is balanced by leaving the schedule more fluid later in the week. Any must-dos and want-to-dos should be finished by end-of-day Thursday. This leaves Friday as the default back-up slot for anything that comes up or runs over from earlier in the week. To honor the intention of the rule, Friday doesn't get given away until you are in it or are absolutely sure you won't need the time for something else. That way, when things go wrong, there is no need to borrow time from the week that follows, because that week will no doubt have crises of its own.

Other people who've tried this Friday approach have found it useful. Maggie Carter, a Tranquility by Tuesday participant who works in marketing, leads a team of ten people. Despite the number of check-ins that management tends to involve, she does her best to keep Fridays open by consciously nudging these meetings to other days.

"Time feels a little more spacious" on Fridays, she says. She can finish expense reports, if that's what she needs to do, but also, "you can follow a thread." She reads articles to the end. She reaches out to people whose names pop into her brain when she's not dialing into a new call every thirty minutes. In this open space, she recently figured out a potential guest for her organization's podcast. On another Friday, she decided to analyze the year's new clients and put together a report. "That would not have happened if I didn't have the Friday afternoon back-up slot," she says. "It's just been a time for creativity and visioning and being a little more strategic in the big picture."

I should stress here that aiming to keep Friday open does not mean that Friday will always *stay* open. To encourage Tranquility by Tuesday participants to find open space in their schedules, I asked them to think about what they might do with this open time if their weeks went perfectly and they didn't need a back-up slot. This may have been people's favorite question in the whole study. Smiley faces bedecked the answers as people fantasized about their spa days, or even just a long and uninterrupted cup of coffee in a favorite chair—which then led to disappointment when the back-up slot had to be used for something else. This is true even though the crisis-averting "something else" is what it was designed for.

So here's my take: If you are fantasizing about a spa day or an uninterrupted cup of coffee, please schedule these things into your life. And then create back-up slots too. I promise it will all fit. As you build the habit of creating a resilient schedule, there will be fewer crises, and more space will open up. Then you can use this space however you want.

Perfection isn't possible, but progress is

Practically, putting four spots in your schedule to go to the gym means you're highly likely to make it to three. If three was the goal, now you feel successful, rather than feeling like a failure when you schedule three spots and make it to only two (or one). Building in open space means you're more likely to make it through your to-do list. All of this creates tranquility right there.

The deeper goal, however, is to build a life that is at least partially inoculated against the common lament that "something came up."

Versions of this explanation pop up everywhere. There was traffic! The Zoom connection didn't work. A podcast guest never dialed in. That weird rash necessitated a trip to urgent care.

Of course something came up. The truth is that life never

does go perfectly. Sometimes I wish I lived in other people's worlds, where there is never traffic, children can always find their shoes, no one gets sick in any form (let alone winding up in the ER), a recipe takes the exact length of time it says it will, and clients never come back with additional questions that have to be addressed *right this very minute*. One might say the people who believe these things are optimists, but a schedule where nothing unexpected happens is also one where old friends never appear in town for a day because of a canceled flight, or you never meet your dream client at a conference and get an invitation to come visit their headquarters this week. Where do you put these things? I imagine most people would find a spot, but then something else has to go, or get pushed forward. Weeks turn into years and at some point you never do think about that business plan you keep meaning to write.

When you imagine that life will go perfectly or at least go as planned, any small event—good or bad—can derail your goals. Any given explanation for such derailment sounds reasonable, and yet many of the things that "come up," and that people hold out as legitimate excuses, are entirely foreseeable.

I know that sounds harsh, but when you assume that something will come up, and you build in space to deal with that, then schedule woes hold less power over your life. You are still empowered to make progress on your goals and to do things that make you happy. When your assistant announces that he is quitting, you have Friday available to start looking through resumes and so you don't have to sacrifice the Thursday afternoon spot you carved out to work on designing your new training program. You have time to do both.

It is hard to overstate the sense of calm this can create—the calm Elizabeth spoke of feeling once she knew her husband was OK and she realized she could still submit her article on time (even early!). The best way to describe this tranquility is that it is the equivalent of going through life with piles of cash in the bank. Break your phone? No worries. If it can't be repaired, you replace it—this afternoon, if you'd like. When you burn dinner, you order pizza. Little things lose their power to bother you. No one can actually accumulate time in the same way that you can build up capital, but having space in a schedule is the psychological equivalent of sitting on a large emergency fund.

I want that sense of wealth for everyone. To play off the title of entrepreneur Rachel Rodgers's personal finance book called *We Should All Be Millionaires*, I think we should all be *time millionaires*. Resilient schedules help us see time as abundant, not scarce.

Participant perspectives: Identifying obstacles

The Tranquility by Tuesday participants were a bit more wary of this rule than some of the others (it had one of the highest proportions of people indicating that the rule was "not right for me" or that it would need to be modified). That said, when I asked if people had needed to skip something fun or important in the last week because something else came up, only about a quarter said this *hadn't* happened. For those who had missed out, the majority indicated that they'd had to skip personal priorities like exercise, hobbies, or family time. Those who'd had to skip professional priorities listed focused work, learning experiences, or making progress on a long-term project. As one person wrote, "work demands seem to run over everything like a truck," and another noted that "there seem to be perpetual crises."

I asked people to think about what activities might best benefit from a back-up slot, and where they could put this back-up slot, or a few hours of open space more generally. I asked them to anticipate any challenges they might encounter in building in a back-up slot, and the reasons they gave explained some of their wariness.

One person confessed to an actual "horror vacui"—that is, a fear of leaving empty space. While I was surprised by the fancy phrase (it turns out to be an art term), I'm not surprised by the impulse. When life is packed full, it can feel wrong to leave time open. There is "so much to do, so little time," one person said, and so it "feels slightly unrealistic to get everything done and keep slots clear." One person wrote of the "Social pressure to accept meeting invitations and feeling like it's wrong to decline things when you technically have nothing else going on."

If someone has been trying to meet with you for four weeks, and you see that Friday morning is open, it's hard to say no again.

But I would argue that you don't truly have "nothing else going on." The empty space serves a purpose. It is not a rude in-
dulgence. No one in the study wound up using their back-up slot
for a golf game in the middle of a busy week, thus leaving work
short-staffed. Instead, building in a back-up slot, or open space
generally, means acknowledging that we do not know, at the beginning of the week, all the tasks that we will need or want to
deal with by the end of the week. By building in space for these
"known unknowns," to borrow the late Donald Rumsfeld's phrase,
you keep them from displacing other things that you have committed to making happen.

I came across one of the best examples of this phenomenon
in Sendhil Mullainathan and Eldar Shafir's book, *Scarcity: Why
Having Too Little Means So Much*. The two professors described
an acute-care Missouri hospital where the operating rooms were
booked at 100 percent capacity. Whenever someone needed emergency surgery, a not-infrequent event in medicine, the hospital
had to bump other, long-scheduled surgeries. Doctors often waited
several hours for an operating room to open up, and sometimes
operated at 2 a.m.—not the best time for anyone to hold a scalpel
if there are other options.

An outside advisor proposed this solution: Leave one operating room unscheduled. To many, this seemed crazy at first. The
facility was already overbooked, and now they were supposed to
reduce capacity further? But it worked. The authors wrote that
on the surface, the hospital lacked operating rooms, but what it

actually lacked was the ability to accommodate emergencies. Since planned procedures were taking up all the rooms, the inevitable unplanned surgeries meant constantly rearranging the schedule— which had "serious repercussions for costs and even quality of care." Once a room was set aside for unscheduled surgeries, all the other rooms could operate on schedule. The hospital managed to handle more surgeries overall, while massively reducing delays.

Participant perspectives: Creatively overcoming challenges

Participants who grasped this potential upside of slack found creative ways to incorporate the equivalent of an empty operating room into their schedules—and not booking that space unless it truly was an emergency. In general, this involved some pointed calendar triage.

"By planning my week on Fridays I have to confront all the things I've agreed to complete this week, and my schedule always looks very full," one person wrote. "This makes it easier during the week to say 'my week is already full' or 'I can do it, but it will have to wait until at least next week' whenever a new project or task comes my way."

Another wrote of cutting out all meetings that did not involve this person's active participation. As another respondent put it, "some meetings are mandatory, but there are some I volunteer to join. So I can stop volunteering so much!"

One person even went so far as to document every meeting with the goal of reducing this number.

"Obviously they're all in my calendar, but I wanted to write them down to underscore the volume, and to identify who can own these instead of me, or where I can go 1–2 times/week vs. every day," this person wrote. The discovery: "I have 9 daily meetings—every day. At that point I got too irritated to bother writing down my 2+ times/week meetings, let alone one-offs. So I'm spending a good bit of my preplanning time this week being deliberate and ruthless about what meetings I need to attend."

Some people, like Elizabeth, wound up booking additional hours of childcare, or asking a partner or relative to cover an additional shift.

Not everyone struggled with the idea of creating open space— a few folks who worked limited hours, or were retired, or who lived alone, described having quite a bit of available space—but for most people, the "when" wasn't an easy question. It turned out to be, however, a worthwhile question.

The results

Despite the general wariness, most respondents indicated in the follow-up survey that they did schedule a back-up slot, or included more open space in their weeks. Doing so had positive effects, such as a massive reduction in time anxiety:

♦ "It felt freeing. It removed an unnecessary sense of pressure from other days."
♦ "It was nice knowing that when something didn't work out, I had a place to turn to, and know that I could still get the task accomplished."
♦ "I've felt less frantic about getting through my to-do list each day."

When stuff came up, it could be dealt with—and that includes positive surprises too.

"I had an unexpected visit from my brother during the workday," one person wrote. "Because I knew I had white space built into my calendar later in the week, I didn't worry about the change in schedule."

Some people found that this deceptively simple rule to create more margin opened their eyes to how close to the edge they had been operating. They hadn't even realized that they were living paycheck to paycheck where time was concerned. One person who wrote of feeling less irritated when people interrupted her mentioned that "sometimes I felt *too* relaxed. I was productive during most of the time though. I think maybe I am just so used to constantly being stressed that I regard anything else as abnormal."

It truly is a mindset shift. So if you have been feeling on edge, and like you never get to your important-but-not-urgent priorities, or you end each week feeling more behind than when you started, try building a back-up slot into your schedule. You might be surprised at the effect.

One scientist who participated in my study wrote, "Yesterday I was all ready to fill this out and tell you that building open space didn't work for me and that it just made me feel like I was wasting time at work because I wasn't maximally fitting in every experiment I could into every minute." But then, "right before I left work yesterday, I realized that I had been wrongly analyzing some data and needed time to go back and correct that data from the past few months. Good thing I had set aside some open space Friday afternoon!"

The main effect, this person wrote, is that she was able to end the week with everything checked off without working extra hours. She was able to spend her weekend enjoying the lovely spring weather, rather than playing catch-up from her previous mistake.

When we create back-up slots, we get things done and get to enjoy our time off. It really is as easy as that.

Take the next step

◆

MAKE BACK-UP PLANS

Creating back-up slots can help us make progress toward our goals, no matter what life throws at us. But sometimes, despite our best efforts, our first-choice goals will not be achievable. When Option A disappears, life feels entirely different if you have a serviceable Option B. If you want to achieve true tranquility, get in the habit of making back-up plans.

The COVID-19 pandemic provided a crash course in this thinking at a fortunate moment when a lot more real Option Bs were available. If you can't meet or celebrate in person, you can now do so virtually. It's not quite the same, but it's not terrible either, with no risk of getting stuck in O'Hare, as those of us who had Zoom Pro accounts before March 2020 could have attested. If you can't take that European vacation you'd planned on, you can go explore the best trails within fifty miles of your home. You can buy tickets for so many socially distanced candy-and-costume focused events that the kids don't even notice that they never went trick-or-treating.

Transferring this philosophy to life as the world recovers means simply thinking through the next best choice. As you make your plans, ponder what else you might do that would work almost as well, and that would take much of the sting out of any disappointment.

This is easy enough in low-stakes situations. Rather than twiddling your thumbs and arguing about options when rain washes out that picnic at the beach, you've already agreed to go to the science museum, which everyone also loves. Adventures and happy memories still ensue.

The real breakthroughs, though, come from creating back-up plans for high-stakes matters, such as your career or education.

For instance, do you have a back-up job plan? That is, a really good idea of what you'd do if you couldn't or did not want to do your current job anymore? The goal of professional networking is not collecting business cards. It's making sure you've got a few folks in different places who've said, "Hey, if you're ever thinking of leaving your job, call me first." Then, if you do need to leave your job, or you're forced out, you've got choices. The existence of these choices means you can take more risks and draw stricter boundaries about what you will and won't do in Option A, your current job—thus improving that experience. So it's worth building your professional relationships to create this same resilience that's desirable in a schedule.

The same is true for the process of college admissions. People sometimes refer to "safety schools" disparagingly, but there is real peace in knowing you will absolutely get a great education. It may be at one place, or it may be at another, but it will happen.

Accepting that a first choice might not happen nudges you to really think through other options, ultimately creating a sense of tranquility. When you know you'll be OK, and sometimes might be a lot better than OK, you can become less attached to any set of events. You maintain your sense of autonomy, whatever happens. Life is ultimately unknowable. But we can make the most of it in any case.

Ask what could go right

Had enough pessimism? I'll throw in a second bonus tip. Yes, time-management masters get in the habit of asking what could go wrong. But it's also helpful to fantasize about what could go fabulously *right*. That way you are prepared to seize opportunities.

So carve out some time—and a back-up slot!—to think this through. If the CEO of your company heard about your great work and offered to put you in charge of any project, what would you ask for? Let's say you randomly posted something online that went viral. Publishers and producers are begging to set up meetings with you. What would you like to create with your new platform? A mysterious great aunt you've never met dies having set up a foundation that will give away $50 million per year, and she's put you in charge of directing it. What causes would you like to support generously?

I'm not saying any of this will happen. I'm almost certain it won't. But if you find yourself thinking that you would love to commission a new symphony with your foundation's funds, this insight can help you figure out how to become more involved in the new music scene now. Maybe you'll be thinking of this desire when you spot a poster at your local university looking for singers to workshop new choral compositions. You won't just walk by. You'll write the information down. You'll call to sign up—and just like that, you'll be on your way to all sorts of new adventures.

Your turn

———————————◆———————————

CREATE A BACK-UP SLOT

Planning questions:

1. Think back over the past week. Have you had to skip something fun or important because something else came up? What was the priority, and what came up?

2. Look to the upcoming week. When could you build at least two hours of open space into your life? Identify a primary spot. Identify a secondary spot.

3. What challenges might keep you from building open space into your life?

4. How can you address these challenges?

5. If life went perfectly, what would you use your open
   time for?

Implementation questions:

1. When were the back-up slots that you built into your
   schedule?

2. What effects did you see in your life from building open
   space into your schedule?

3. What challenges did you face while implementing this week's
   strategy?

4. How did you address these challenges?

5. If you needed to modify this rule, how did you do so?

6. How likely are you to continue using this rule in your life?

RULE 6

One Big Adventure,
One Little Adventure

We don't ask "where did the time go?"
when we remember where the time went.

ertain days stand out in the mind more than others. I have
thought a great many times about a late June day in 2006.
My husband Michael and I were traveling around the bright-at-
all-hours Norwegian countryside, partly as background for a sus-
pense novel I was writing (no, you haven't read it), but mostly for
fun. To celebrate the beginning of summer, we decided to try one
of Norway's most popular hikes. We would take a boat to the
trailhead, wind our way up a photogenic stone ridge to the peak,
then come down the back side of the mountain to our hotel.

It seemed easy enough, though we were smart enough to bring jackets and wear long pants. Weather changes swiftly in the mountains. I don't think I appreciated how swiftly. As we began ascending the stone scramble, our summer day turned cold and rainy. I also realized that Norwegians have a different sense of what constitutes a general-interest hike than Americans. The trail wound up on small, slippery rock outcroppings measuring a few feet across with thousand-foot plunges on either side.

Did I mention my fear of heights?

So I kept my eyes on the top, trying not to look down as the mountain went in and out of the clouds. I paced myself through each step, hoping the trail would ease up soon. And yes, it did level off. But as we reached the peak, the rain turned into snow. Lots of snow. A real honest-to-goodness June blizzard. We were soon lost and hunting for trail markers that had completely disappeared in this frigid mountaintop snowfield.

Looking back on that icy summer day now, it seems obvious that eventually we would be on the other side of the experience. It was a popular hike, with more boats arriving every few hours. If fewer people were coming down than going up, someone was going to notice. Yet in the moment, surrounded by disorienting white, all I could think was that we were going to be there forever.

Finally, after what seemed like ages but was probably less than half an hour of being lost in the blizzard, we found a crew of equally lost Norwegian soldiers who were hiking on their leave. One had a compass; we used that to navigate our way across the peak through dead reckoning. We emerged on the calmer side of the mountain, where, after some hunting, we spotted trail markers. The clouds cleared. We could see down to the valley, accessible by a pleasant stroll through subarctic meadows of boulders and microscopic flowers. I ate dinner at my hotel. My only physical memory of that snowstorm was that my slightly frozen fingers tingled for three days afterward.

Still, those few hours of gripping the rocks and then being lost in the summer snow are carved in my memory. Though they happened many years ago, I remember small details—something I cannot say about the equivalent volume of hours between yesterday's lunch and dinner, which I am certain will *not* lodge in my memory. I've mostly forgotten that span of time already. Those hours were fleeting, while the hours on that mountaintop had heft.

Why is that?

I suppose it seems obvious. Seconds tick forward with the steady beat of a metronome, and yet we experience time in vastly changing ways depending on what we've done with it. These differences have important implications for how we should structure our time to feel thicker and richer in more ordinary circumstances.

As I've studied time perception, I've learned that intensity in any form creates deep memories. That is logical enough. Our brains are busy; we hold on only to what nudges us from complacence. More intriguing is that our sense of how swiftly time is passing is then shaped by how many memories we have formed.

Our brains perceive a general background pace of memory-making—let's say six memories to the fortnight. When that pace accelerates, and we have more memories of any given unit of time, the time feels longer. This explains why the first day of a trip to somewhere exotic can feel like a month. In a completely new environment, your brain has no idea what it will need to know, and so it is holding on to all of it, laying down a dozen memories before lunch, and thus slowing the progression of time.

This phenomenon also explains why time seems to accelerate as we grow older. Adolescence and young adulthood feature much novelty: new schools, new cities, new jobs, new loves. All is unknown, so the background pace of memory-making is swifter than it will ever be again. This makes time, in memory, seem expansive. Middle age, on the other hand, lists toward routine. The background pace of memory-making can stall completely as each day seems much like the last. Each weekday morning is the same chaos of getting the kids on the bus, getting to work, slogging through meetings and a teeming inbox, returning home to dinner, baths, bedtime, and the television. We tend not to get lost on Norwegian mountaintops, but we don't nudge ourselves toward beneficial risks either.

Perhaps that sounds depressing, but it doesn't need to be. Once we emerge from that shaken snow globe of youth and settle down, we simply have to consciously create positive intensity in our lives—so whole years don't disappear into memory sinkholes, measured only in the changing heights of children.

The good news is that this doesn't require hiking in summer-solstice blizzards, or even ditching the routines that make good choices automatic. We simply need to find ways to introduce novelty into day-to-day life. Novelty creates memories. Memories expand time. We don't ask "Where did the time go?" when we remember where the time went.

This brings us to **Tranquility by Tuesday Rule 6: One big adventure, one little adventure**. Each week, aim to plan one larger adventure and one smaller one into your schedule. Doing so can change the entire experience of time, creating memories and an ongoing sense of hope.

Before anyone complains that they cannot fathom weekly excursions to another continent, let me clarify some definitions:

- A big adventure means something that requires a few hours—think half a weekend day.
- A little adventure could take just an hour or so, and fit on a lunch break or a weekday evening, as long as it is something out of the ordinary.

These adventures should be things you genuinely want to do, or at least want to have done, a distinction we'll get to later in this chapter.

So, for example, as I look back on my time logs for a few summer weeks, some big adventures have included a family beach trip to Ocean Grove in New Jersey (with a stop for ice cream afterward, of course), going to a Phillies game with my husband, taking the big kids peach and blueberry picking at an orchard about an hour away, and taking my daughter to that chocolate-themed amusement destination known as Hersheypark. Some little adventures have included taking a different child out for a sushi lunch at a restaurant where we sat low to the ground, going down a water slide, seeing a rather unexpected collection of sculptures featuring nylon stockings at the Philadelphia Museum of Art, and taking a family walk in a garden we'd never visited before.

In the years I have been teaching this rule, I have found it has a few benefits.

1. To plan two adventures each week, **we have to plan our weeks.**

This reinforces the weekly planning habit we learned in the second chapter, with a satisfying emphasis on planning what we *want* to do, and not just what we need to do.

2. This habit **builds regular doses of anticipation** into our mental landscapes.

People who plan one big adventure and one little adventure each week aren't just waiting for vacations to do interesting and enjoyable things. They have something to look forward to every three to four days!

3. We start to see that **even small bits of time can make memories.**

A regular Tuesday can be transformed without transforming our whole lives. This combination of one big adventure and one little adventure will make weeks feel interesting, but isn't going to exhaust or bankrupt anyone, or unsettle the good routines that do exist. Go to worship services every weekend? Great. A half-day big adventure can still fit alongside that commitment. Have lunch with a different direct report most weekdays? Amazing. You can still visit that nearby sculpture garden some evening after work.

This formula of one big adventure and one little adventure makes time feel somewhat like a song with a key change between verses. The comforting melody is still there; your awareness simply rises with the pitch.

Participant perspectives: Ideas for implementation

After sharing this rule with the Tranquility by Tuesday participants, I asked them to think about what big adventure and little adventure they could have in the upcoming week. If they already had any big or little adventures on the calendar, I asked them to note these, so they could savor and appreciate them—consciously committing them to memory, rather than barreling through.

Most people were game to try. While a small number felt like their lives were adventurous enough, the more common initial hurdle was figuring out what to do. In a busy life, coming up with adventures can feel like one more thing on the to-do list, let alone figuring out when you'll do them, though the answer to this, ironically, is to make *more* lists. When you have lists of practical adventures that you've dreamed up over time, you don't have to think them up in the moment.

So carve out a few minutes over the next week to think about this question of what you'd like to do. If you made a List of 100 Dreams (from Chapter 2), this will likely contain some doable adventures alongside that three-week jaunt to Fiji. Ask friends and family members for their ideas. I post seasonal fun lists on my blog (lauravanderkam.com) with both big and little adventures that celebrate each specific time of year. The winter fun list might include ice skating at the outdoor rink downtown, and sledding down a local hill. A recent spring fun list included doing a hummingbird-themed thousand-piece puzzle, picking tulips at Holland Ridge Farms in New Jersey, and taking thirty pictures of thirty depictions of flowers at an art museum. Some items repeat year to year, but doing something once a year or so can still feel adventurous, and the more I make these lists, the more aware I become of things that might make life a little more exciting.

Multiple survey participants used the week's prompt to begin their own lists.

"You can't plan what you don't know about!" one person wrote, so "I checked some online calendars to look for possible events and activities."

Another person decided to set aside some time at the end of each month to look for potential events in the next month, and another wrote of creating an ongoing list in her digital planner. "I think remembering a certain activity I want to do three months from now is hard, so I'm hoping already having it as an option on my calendar will help," she wrote.

The simple act of devoting mental space to this question can get the ideas flowing; "Every time I encounter one thing as a potential adventure, it tends to spur another thought in my brain to look up information on a related idea," one person wrote. "Sometimes these spiral, and I end up with several options."

To be sure, the COVID restrictions some participants were still experiencing in the spring of 2021 made following this rule more challenging. Erratic weather can put a damper on adventure (even if other participants scored some gorgeous spring sunshine), and the presence of babies and toddlers can, as one participant wrote, make adventures seem like "more work than fun." I certainly sympathize with this last sentiment. A day trip to the beach can involve more than an hour of packing diapers and extra clothes and snacks and towels and then sunscreening five children, to say nothing of the complaints that flow, inevitably, from the truth that nothing is ever fun for the whole time for the whole family. Sometimes, you wonder why you bother.

I'll talk more about the "why" later in this chapter, but it's also helpful to realize **that adventure is more a state of mind than an objective standard of measurement**. If your family is excited about that trip to a new gelato place, then that is an adventure, even if someone else's bar for adventure is sailing like a Viking around the Norwegian fjords. When life is limited for one reason or another, be that because of pandemic rules, or health issues, or a lack of funds or childcare, we can simply focus on adventures that are possible, rather than those that aren't. Watching a lightning storm from a covered porch is an adventure. Climbing a backyard tree you've never climbed before is an adventure. During the strictest days of lockdowns, we could still explore our local trails and so our weekly "big adventure" tended to be a weekend family walk. We tried cuisines from different restaurants. I listened to online lectures about Bach's B-minor mass, and attended Zoom toasts for friends' books. One participant described "two hours spent in the woods building bridges over a tiny stream out of moss and twigs and rocks with my kids. Well . . . that there is a big adventure in lockdown."

You can also recast something you were *already* doing as an adventure, or tweak it to boost the novelty factor. If you regularly walk with a friend, choose a new route, with a stop at a new café to finish your chat afterward. A grocery store trip could become an adventure by turning it into a family competition (who can finish their portion of the list first?) or by adding a stop at an international grocery store or a farmer's market. If you work from home, you'll take breaks at some point, so why not use one for a fifteen-minute bike ride? As one participant wrote, "I discovered that it doesn't take much right now to provide a little escape from ordinary life—window shopping downtown and ice cream, a drive to a neighboring town to check out a new park and pick up take-out from a restaurant that is new to us."

Plans turn desires into reality

With their mission to plan one big adventure and one little adventure, my study participants enjoyed all sorts of wonderful intensity in their weeks. They . . .

- Planted apple trees.
- Participated in a virtual improv show.
- Played the part of the narrator in a Holy Week church service.
- Bought and installed a slide in the backyard.
- Dreamed up an elaborate April Fool's joke.
- Took the kids out for ice cream on the first day the ice cream parlor opened for the summer season.
- Took an evening walk to see the spring blooms.
- Organized their first group playdate at a playground since COVID began.
- Held an outdoor princess party for a child and her friends.
- Took a sunrise walk around a city harbor during a work trip.

- Visited a sculpture park in a nearby city.
- Started a wine club with friends, which this participant described as a "book club without books."

One participant even got married during this week of the study, which is definitely memorable, though obviously not inspired by this rule!

A wedding is hopefully a once-in-a-lifetime event, but for many other adventures, "In a way these activities weren't so out of the ordinary. I theoretically would have done them if I hadn't 'planned' them," one person wrote, "but because I had planned, I definitely did. I felt full and happy afterward."

Plans turn desires into reality. This insight explains why some people found a silver lining in the COVID-era capacity restrictions that many attractions still had in effect. In the past, you could have decided on a Saturday morning to spend the morning at the zoo, and gone when you felt like it, or—as often happens—not have gone, if it seemed like a bother. With the need to make a timed reservation, a general desire to go to the zoo turned into a ticket with a time on the schedule. This made it far more likely to happen.

People definitely enjoyed their adventures, including the events themselves, the anticipation, and the reflection. Appreciating this three-part emotional experience of any event can help you stretch out the enjoyment of the event itself. A person who planned a celebration noted that "it was fun talking with my family about highlights from the party," with these shared recollections making it feel "like it lasted longer."

Even changing up a lunch break could, in a way, be life-changing. "I didn't imagine that a simple break in weekdays could be so nice," one person wrote. Planning in a midday browsing session at a local bookshop, and knowing this was how the lunch hour would be spent, made the entire morning feel full of expectation and possibility, even if in reality it was full of meetings.

Participant perspectives:
Identifying (and overcoming) challenges

There were challenges too. Planning anything can feel extravagant if life feels chaotic. "Big adventures feel more daunting when I'm in survival mode," one person wrote.

In the middle of busy workweeks, people wondered where they would find the time. This can be challenging, but it's helpful to remember that work tends to expand to fill the available space. If you spend three hours on Saturday having an adventure, or one hour on a Wednesday evening, your email will still be there afterward. Indeed, I'd venture it will still be there in the same quantity as it would be whether the adventures happened or not. This is true for housework and errands too. Best to make the memories and let email and chores fill in around them.

Another common challenge was that people's partners or other family members sometimes resisted—either a specific proposed adventure, or adventures more generally. If Dad wants to take the family hiking to see the fall leaves, and Mom wants to stay home every weekend and do "nothing," how does this play out?

When it comes to planning specific adventures, it might help to make sure that all family members' ideas get considered. A combination adventure (new playground *plus* a farmer's market, or a bike ride *plus* pumpkin pancakes at a diner) can work more people's desires into the schedule.

There is also wisdom in recognizing that other adults can do what they want. They don't have to participate, but they also can't force you to do "nothing." Have your adventure, taking along any kids too young to take care of themselves or setting them up at playdates or activities, and enjoy your time. When you make and share your good memories, sometimes other people become more interested. Their desire to do "nothing" wasn't a deeply held philosophical position. It was more a matter of general fatigue. If that is the case, you can make sure that all adults in the family are getting their own restorative time—which we'll cover in the next chapter—so adventures don't draw on a dry well.

I'd also recommend a sense of perspective: One three-hour big adventure planned on a weekend afternoon after everyone's games and practices are done still leaves a lot of open time. There are approximately thirty-six waking hours between 6 p.m. Friday and 6 a.m. Monday. Even if you have kids' activities, religious commitments, and other things going on, there is going to be downtime. The question is just how much. One big adventure and one little adventure creates a good balance. The weekend can feel memorable, and still not come close to being exhausting.

How to overcome your own inertia

To me, the most poignant challenge was not any of the standard logistical hassles. People learned to get timed tickets to events, and to book babysitters for adults-only adventures. They looked for free events when budgets were tight. Instead, what sometimes happened was that people would think up adventures, plan them in, and then find them hard to do in the moment.

"Inertia is always a little bit of a challenge," one person wrote. "It's easier to *not* do things than to do them."

Another person dispatched with potentially conflicting work obligations, but then succumbed to the temptation to do "nothing" once the moment arrived: "I'm such a creature of habit it was hard to deviate from the norm."

Another looked at the hurdles between desire and execution and confessed to saying "let's stay home."

I get it. You planned to peruse that cool art store in a nearby historic neighborhood on a Wednesday evening. But then Wednesday evening arrives and you're tired, and kind of hungry, and it looks like there might be traffic, plus your colleague reminds you that it's always hard to park in that historic neighborhood, and you realize it would be far easier to drive straight home from work. You wake up on Saturday morning with plans to load the bikes onto the car for an excursion to a scenic trail you read about that's an hour away, but no one is exactly moving quickly. Getting to the trail is going to require a ton of effort, to say nothing of overcoming the anxiety that trying anything untried can cause.

I had this exact conversation with myself one February night when I had bought tickets to take my big kids skating at the outdoor ice rink downtown (it was on my Winter Fun List). The day dawned snowy enough that the rink closed for my ticket window. Management promised that the tickets would be honored later that night once the snow stopped and the plows came through, but of course that meant I would be driving downtown on slippery roads. As I pondered street parking on roads covered with snow drifts, and getting four kids into rental ice skates, and figuring out what we would do with our stuff, the whole thing felt like a lot of trouble. Why not just pour myself a glass of wine and read a magazine? I follow a great many minimalist-focused Instagram accounts that would recommend such an evening as restorative self-care. My house was nice and warm. Everyone would have been content to watch YouTube all evening.

But I knew that was my present, experiencing self talking. The "self," as we think of the autobiographical narrative running through our brains, is really three selves. There is the "anticipating self," who looked forward to that ice skating trip, the "experiencing self," who would do it, and the "remembering self" (a concept Nobel Prize–winning psychologist Daniel Kahneman popularized in his research), who would look back fondly on the memory of those kids zipping around on the ice.

We can see the tension here. The anticipating self gets to don the identity of "cool mom who is going to take her kids ice skating." The remembering self gets to enjoy the memory. It is the experiencing self who actually has to get up off the couch, get misdirected by her GPS to the bus circle above the rink parking lot, and fumble with the change machine to score quarters for her shoe locker rental. This can seem like an unfair division of labor.

But because few things produce nonstop bliss through the entire process, it is a mistake to indulge all the experiencing self's whims. She is one part of a trio. She should not get veto power. Indeed, once the initial resistance is conquered, the experiencing self will probably enjoy things too. People tend to go ice skating because it's fun. To qualify as an adventure, something needs to be enjoyable, awe-inspiring, meaningful, or at least generate a really good story for parties. All of these are worth experiencing in life alongside the wine-and-YouTube routine.

So I employed my favorite mental trick that makes anything tough more doable: **Picture yourself on the other side**.

In the abstract, our brains consider our future selves to be strangers. We're naturally less concerned about future needs than current ones. But if you actively picture Future You, this tendency shifts, and you can make better decisions. Some research has suggested that when people see renderings of themselves at future ages, they're marginally more likely to save for retirement.

But honestly, you don't need to look years into the future to change your decision rubric. Often, very little stands between us and being on the other side of something. We're talking hours, not years. The essence of discipline is recognizing that this mild discomfort tends to be a small price to pay for the upside to Future You. Putting your feet on the cold floor when the alarm goes off in the morning isn't easy, but if you've returned from your morning run charged up for the day every other morning when you've gone for a run, most likely Future You will experience this same energy boost. You just have to picture yourself forty-five minutes later—or even experiencing that runner's high fifteen minutes into your sunrise run—and push through.

I know that discipline isn't exactly a fun concept, but this skill of picturing yourself on the other side is actually instrumental to happiness, and making time for what matters, which is the point of this "One big adventure, one little adventure" rule. Often, happiness takes effort. We'll return to the concept of "effortful fun" in Chapter 9, but for now, we just need to remember that making memories requires novelty or intensity. Both of these can push us outside of our comfort zones, and might involve a little anxiety. If we let mild discomfort dissuade us, we will cut ourselves off from many things that will make us feel, looking back, like we have escaped the slog and led a rich and full life.

So on that snowy February night, I pictured myself on the other side of the ice skating adventure. I knew that in a few hours I would be in my warm bed. I'd probably even get home in time to read a magazine with a glass of wine if I wanted to. Time passes one way or another. It always passes. There is nothing you can do to stop it. In a few hours I could have gone ice skating, or I could have not gone ice skating, but probably, as I climbed under the covers, I would prefer to have the memory of those lights around the rink as they reflected against the ice and the dark sky. Yes, the night would take energy. But really, what was I saving my energy for?

If you want to do something, most likely you will be happy to have done it. Probably you will enjoy vast chunks of the adventure itself too.

The results

This was certainly the experience of the Tranquility by Tuesday participants who followed through on their adventures. "We definitely made memories!" one happy person wrote. Another said that "Life feels more expansive, and I feel more connected with my family," with a third feeling "more rejuvenated and less bitter to tackle a very busy week ahead at work."

At the end of the study, and one month after, participants rated "One big adventure, one little adventure" as one of the more beneficial rules, even as it was also near the top of the scale for being the most difficult to do. For many people, following this rule did involve some major changes to how they planned out their weeks. "As a homebody, I'd rather stay at home and then I end up not doing anything fun," one person said. So, "Even if it's just one adventure a week, I've been purposefully choosing things to do—walking our city's canal path with a friend, going to the farmer's market to buy some plants, and going to a baseball game at our city's minor league baseball stadium."

Making these purposeful choices made life a lot more interesting. A participant who called this "my favorite new habit" wrote, at the one-month follow-up, of deciding to accompany her young adult daughter, who was working remotely for a law firm, to San Juan, Puerto Rico, even though she had only a short window of time. "We flew down on Wednesday and I was back home by Sunday at midnight, but in between we had a jam-packed time of sightseeing art museums and historical sites, sitting on the beach, going to a neighborhood church, taking the ferry to another site, seeing flamenco dancers, eating ice cream for breakfast, and all the things you do with a twenty-six-year-old adventurer!" This mother noted that "it was a wonderful memory and such a lesson that even small amounts of time can yield big adventures and excitement if you plan for it," and that "It makes life so much more colorful and fun to inject a little excitement and novelty into the routine of ordinary days!"

When all life feels the same, there is nothing to distinguish days from one another, but even little adventures can change this perception. "Having adventures built in my schedule gives me a sense of time—'the week in which I did this and that'—in comparison to the weeks that just pass by similar to the ones before," one person wrote. Another found that "time seemed to slow down a bit as I savored the fun."

Adventures even shifted people's perception of themselves. They were adventurous! "Time stretches and the inner narrative changes," one person wrote. Perhaps life doesn't have to be all toil; perhaps adulthood isn't defined by the tedium of watching the clock. One person wrote of trying on this intriguing new feeling that "we were the kind of people who do fun stuff." Another welcomed the chance to think about "taking up space for joy in my own life and in my family's calendar—like, I get to play too! My value does not subsist in my work! What I want my life to look like matters!"

It does matter. Joy matters, and we, as the master artists crafting our schedules, can weave joy into the tapestry of time. That is a good-enough reason to plan one big adventure and one little adventure into each week, though as the adventures stack up, we can come to know the deeper reason for this rule. Life changes when you know that hundreds, if not thousands, of future adventures are waiting for you. Every day feels full of possibility. This mere sense of possibility, in itself, can leave you open to more adventures. Some participants noted that as they began to feel more adventurous, they began saying yes to things that in the past might not have fit into the rubric of a normal day. An older child mentions going swimming at night. If the pool is open, why not? An evening swim—even if it's just sitting on the side while a preteen paddles around—can change the experience of a Tuesday, as you stare out at the summer sky, the stars, and the fireflies punctuating the darkness like little adventures can punctuate time.

Take the next step

◆

ADD WHIMSY

Planning one big adventure and one little adventure each week can make life feel like less of a grind. But it's not the only way to lighten up, and many of us could use a lot more cheer in the daily experience of our hours.

So, after you've gotten into the rhythm of building in adventures, try adding another component: some weekly note of whimsy too. Whimsy is playfully quaint or fanciful behavior—anything that's a little silly and out-of-the-ordinary. Ask this question: What might make you smile?

With that goal in mind, in our house, we've often made specially shaped and dyed pancakes for minor or made-up holidays: Green four-leaf clovers for St. Patrick's Day, red hearts for Valentine's Day, snowmen for the first snowfall of the year. Holidays in general are great for whimsy. We once made a pilgrimage to the Franklin Institute's giant heart for Valentine's Day. We sometimes celebrate those marketer-designed food holidays like International Waffle Day or National Pretzel Day. Just search online for "food holidays" and start marking your favorites (National Chocolate Fondue Day?) on the calendar.

Maybe there's something you can do to make your usual activities just a bit more memorable. Get matching T-shirts for a family excursion. Print up a silly photo for your desk, and switch it out frequently, or put a vignette outside your home office window (garden gnomes are the epitome of whimsy). Hang a disco ball or a string of lights somewhere in your house—maybe on a little evergreen tree at a time far removed from Christmas. Get one of those adult coloring books with whimsical patterns. Paint your nails an offbeat color; you can paint your toenails if you don't want to share such personal expression with the world. Draw something fun on the driveway with chalk, such as the giant chalk game of Chutes and Ladders one study participant reported creating. Blow bubbles on a break.

None of this is life-changing of course, but when things are different, seeing these fancies can nudge us out of the mindless state that tends to characterize day-to-day life.

Hours always march into the past, but at least they can carry a little whimsy with them as they whistle on their way.

Your turn

---◆---

ONE BIG ADVENTURE,
ONE LITTLE ADVENTURE

Planning questions:

1. What "big adventures" (taking a few hours) would you like to try in the next month? List at least three.

2. What "little adventures" (taking about an hour) would you like to try in the next month? List at least three.

3. Think about this past week. Did you have any adventures, big or little? What were they?

4. Now look ahead to next week. What big adventure would you like to have next week? Perhaps you already have an

adventure planned; if so, write about that adventure, or share an idea for an additional adventure.

5. When could you experience this big adventure?

6. What little adventure would you like to have next week?

7. When could you experience this little adventure?

8. What obstacles might keep you from having these adventures?

9. How can you address these challenges?

Implementation questions:

1. What big adventure(s) did you experience this week?

2. What little adventure(s) did you experience this week?

3. What effects did you see in your life from doing something out of the ordinary?

4. What challenges, if any, did you face while implementing this week's strategy? Did anything make it difficult for you to plan adventures into your life, or to have the adventures you planned?

5. How did you address these challenges?

6. If you modified this rule, how did you do so?

7. How likely are you to continue using this rule in your life?

Take One Night for You

Committing to fun means the fun happens.

*H*annah Bogensberger has a busy life. She works full-time as a software engineer in Seattle. She has three children, who were all under the age of six when I talked with her about her schedule for the Tranquility by Tuesday project in early 2021. Her husband is an ICU nurse, hardly a low-stress job at any point, and particularly so during the pandemic's various surges.

All of this might suggest a story of having no time for fun. And yet, Hannah told me, on any given Tuesday, you could find her eating a quick dinner after work, and then driving five minutes to a local indoor tennis place. She meets up with two of her sisters, whose presence provides accountability to make sure she comes. They play and chat for an hour.

It's a simple thing, really. A two-mile trip. She's home in time "to do the teeth and the prayers and the whole bedtime routine." And yet, having this one night that she knows is for her, and is separate from her work and family responsibilities, has changed her perspective about her schedule—making her more relaxed, and making time in general more joyful.

"I'm not great, but it's fun, and it's something I look forward to," she says. Physical activity tends to make people feel good—as does laughing with people you've known since childhood—and "during the activity you're so focused on it you're not thinking about the to-do list and other stresses in life." Indeed, the first time she returned home after this bout of tennis tranquility, her husband told her, "You look like you're glowing."

Not bad for a Tuesday, right?

I've been thinking a lot lately about how Hannah described her Tuesdays—not because the idea of a regular Tuesday-night tennis game is so earth-shaking, but because the happiness pay-off for that ninety minutes out of the 168 hours we all have each week is so substantial. Hannah's fun is pretty accessible too. She and her sisters play at a public tennis court. She and her husband trade off kid coverage; one could imagine a similar swap with a neighbor or relative. Absent that, hiring a neighborhood teen to watch the kids for an hour and a half on a Tuesday probably wouldn't break the bank for most people reading this book.

So, given all this glowy anticipation and post-game basking, it raises the question: Why hadn't she done this before? Not everyone likes tennis, or lives near their siblings, but more broadly, why don't more adults commit to the equivalent of an hour or two every Tuesday for something they find genuinely fun?

I know the explanations, and there's no doubt that during the busy years, hobbies and personal passions tend to fall by the wayside. People will sometimes make space for flexible fun like reading, crafting, or solo exercise, and that's great. But committing to something out of the house, and involving other people, that meets at a particular time, seems like an entirely different matter. There are all the logistics to consider. Plus there are other people's schedules, and the question of whether chaos will ensue if we're not actively managing things. Life feels complicated enough as it is.

Hannah has thought about this question too. In the past, when she pondered injecting some scheduled levity into her life, the timing hadn't felt right, or she figured that adding an extra thing to the schedule would simply be too much work. Indeed, even figuring out what she might find enjoyable enough to do every week took a reasonable amount of effort. The tennis facility was close, so that might seem obvious in retrospect, but she hadn't played since a junior varsity adventure decades before. Furthermore, her sisters weren't going to magically show up in the midst of their jam-packed Tuesdays. Like anyone, Hannah wanted to enjoy life, but she needed a practical, straightforward strategy that would nudge her to make this happen.

Fortunately, she signed up for the Tranquility by Tuesday project. And it turned out that **Tranquility by Tuesday Rule 7: Take one night for you** was exactly the nudge she needed.

Building a career—and raising a family—are meaningful activities, but they require a lot of energy. To do our best, we need time we can count on to recharge, apart from these obligations. We need time to do things we find intrinsically energizing for ourselves, as individuals.

So, each week, take one evening (or an equivalent number of hours) off from family and work responsibilities and do something that makes life feel meaningful and fun.

This evening or block of weekend time can be spent as you wish, but ideally, it features a commitment to an activity, like playing on a softball team, being part of a community drama troupe, or, like Hannah, going to a regular meet-up with specific people for a specific purpose. Your commitment to these other people provides accountability. You have a reason to go even when life gets busy. Ideally this activity happens at the same time every week, so you don't need to keep planning it. This time can become, officially, "your time." You don't need to ask permission or work around others' schedules. If it is Tuesday, then you are going to your tennis game. You can look forward to your fun and know that you will come home aglow afterward.

It is hard to overstate the payoff that can come from this rule. One night off can change the entire rhythm of the week. If your night off is Tuesday, you feel more tranquil during a rough

Monday-night bedtime routine, because you know this mini-vacation is coming up. You manage your energy during the Tuesday workday so that you've got plenty for the evening. You think through potential problems and ways you might solve them so you don't miss your commitment for what are not actually good reasons. And then, during the fun, you can just focus on what you're doing. Ideally, this turns down the volume on any family or work woes—from all-consuming to background noise, at least for a little while.

Why we all need a night off

I developed this rule because I have seen the difference it makes in my own life, a difference not dissimilar from the glow Hannah developed. I love to sing. So I've made a habit of seeking out community choirs wherever I live. After moving to New York City in 2002, I joined three ensembles as a way to get my work-from-home-self dressed and out of the apartment at least three evenings per week.

After getting married and starting a family, I winnowed my involvement down to one choir, the Young New Yorkers' Chorus. We met every Tuesday night. I imagine that some of my bar-going fellow young singers were surprised that I elected to sing in a concert two weeks after having my first baby, and that I then kept coming to rehearsals after baby number two as well, but in this time, I had a realization. With an apartment full of little kids, and a husband who worked long hours and traveled, I needed this time away. Tuesday stayed as my night "off" for four years.

When we left New York City, I didn't immediately find a choir I wanted to join in suburban Pennsylvania. So I did other things to approximate a night off, like writing fiction in the local library one night a week. But I missed making music. I missed having this weekly commitment. We joined a church, and I noticed that the choir sounded a number of notches above the average church choir. I started going to their Thursday-night rehearsals. Just like that, Thursday became my night for doing something challenging that is not my job and is not mothering. It is something else entirely.

When I've talked about singing in my choirs, and suggested the idea of taking a night off for a commitment along those lines, I've encountered numerous explanations from people for why it just wouldn't work. I'm always curious about these explanations. Kids are a convenient excuse, but they don't need to be. I have five of them. I work. My husband works. Getting to rehearsals has not been easy. But it is important enough to me that I expect my family's support. Kids do activities like karate and baseball, and Mom does choir. I put it on the activity spreadsheet, right alongside their interests. We arrange childcare for rehearsals when my husband can't cover. I believe that something that brings joy to my life deserves to be a family financial priority. I believe it deserves to be a priority in your family too. In any case, if it came down to this choice, I'd be happy to keep driving my decade-old car perpetually . . . and make it to rehearsals. I don't have perfect attendance, but I have also negotiated to be on earlier flights back from speeches so I can get to Thursday-night rehearsals on time. When I'm swamped with work, I work late on other nights. A fun commitment gives you a reason to stop work at least one night every week, and in talking with other people about their community and personal commitments, I've found that many colleagues come to expect it, even if they grumble at first.

Now the "one night" part of this rule doesn't have to literally be a *night*. If you'd like to volunteer as an online math tutor on Saturday mornings or do twenty-five-mile bike rides with a friend on Sundays, this can work too, as long as all adults in the household have an equal chance to do their chosen activity.

I'd also note that, unlike many of the other Tranquility by Tuesday rules, this rule might be tough to implement immediately. Even if you know that you would love to play the violin in an ensemble again, your local community orchestra probably isn't holding auditions tomorrow. But you can take baby steps. Until you get an audition scheduled, you can carve out an hour to practice the violin, or sign up for lessons.

When you make time for you, you remind yourself of your identity apart from your job and family responsibilities. You are an intriguing and talented person. You make space for what matters. That can make time feel more enjoyable and balanced, and make life feel less like a slog.

Participant perspectives: How to find what makes you glow

After introducing this rule, I asked Tranquility by Tuesday participants if they had regular fun-for-them commitments in their lives. A reasonable number already did, such as book clubs, Bible study groups, a regular fitness class or running group, volunteering gigs, or regular friend get-togethers.

"Every Thursday night I meet up with my two best friends to hang out, watch a movie, support and encourage one another. We started this when we were all freshmen in college and now have been doing it for twenty years!" one person said.

For those who didn't have such commitments, or whose fun activities were irregular or less frequent (e.g., a once-every-month book club), I asked them to think of what they might add in.

While some had readily available answers (e.g., that spiritual small group a person kept meaning to join), others struggled to answer this question:

- "I'm not sure. Through the survey process, I'm realizing that I need to give some more thought to what might be fun."
- "I really don't know, which is probably the crux of the problem. What to do, not when to do it!"
- "It's hard to even comprehend having a night off that isn't for work."

As people brainstormed ideas, their answers often turned into meandering lists: "The first thing that comes to mind is an in-person barre class that I'd be more likely to do during the morning instead of in the evening. Joining a knitting group would be fun, and I'd really like to get back to rowing soon. I rowed from '99 with only a couple breaks until 2018 when I stopped while very pregnant with the boys . . ."

When people feel busy enough, they often don't think about what they'd like to do with their time, which means this question can feel challenging. It's worth listing out all these potential answers, and thinking back to extracurricular activities you did in high school, in college, or as a young adult. Maybe there are options for trying these now. You can look around, do some research, ask friends. You can try different things, such as a four-week adult gymnastics class to see how you like it, or a one-off volunteering stint to see if you'd find value in being part of that organization long-term. There's no need to rush into a decision, which doesn't need to be permanent in any case.

If you give yourself six months to get your new commitment up and running, my guess is that you'll be able to find something that you'll want to do. Or you could start something. I'm happy to report that a few new book clubs and regular friend social events, just like Hannah's tennis game, owe their existence to the Tranquility by Tuesday project!

Fun doesn't need to be flexible

As people thought of this question, a fair number came up with ideas that were not time specific, or that could be done in their homes. These included activities such as doing a yoga video or taking a bubble bath. One person fantasized about watching a show "without feeling guilty about not doing chores." Someone else wanted to spend time making the house cozy. People mentioned baking, doing embroidery, or just being alone: "I'd eat my dinner watching something on Netflix, with no children around me!"

All of these are pleasant ways to spend a few hours. They can certainly work in the short term as a respite from work and family demands. Single parents and those experiencing pandemic lockdowns during the survey had practical reasons for wanting to make their fun more accommodating.

But I'd push back on this idea that, as a parent, or as a person with a demanding career, your fun has to be flexible. It doesn't. There is nothing flexible about an every-Thursday-night rehearsal starting promptly at 7 p.m. in a specific place, but *I don't care.* The problem with being flexible about your fun is that when your fun is flexible it will become contingent on other people not wanting you to do something else. You can take your night . . . as long as work isn't busy. You can take your night . . . as long as your spouse doesn't need to work late. You can take your night . . . as long as your kid doesn't have an extra soccer practice or want you to drive her to the mall. What grounds do you have to argue? You can do your yoga video whenever. Your bathtub isn't going anywhere. So you can in fact turn your evening over to chaperone duties.

The trouble with this bargain is that things that can happen "whenever" have a funny tendency to happen when-*never*. Or at least you don't know when they will happen, so you can't as easily look forward to them. You can't manage your energy toward making them happen, which means that rather than turn on the yoga video when time appears, you turn on HGTV.

If your string quartet practices every Tuesday night at 7:30 p.m., on the other hand, you will build this into your schedule. Everyone else will (eventually) build it into their expectations too. You cover for a colleague on Monday so he covers for you on Tuesday. You organize your week so that anything with a Wednesday deadline gets handled by 6 p.m. Tuesday. Your spouse knows, when she schedules a work dinner on Tuesday, that she will need to make any necessary childcare arrangements (or give you a well-in-advance heads-up that those will be needed if you're the one who normally books such things). The kid who always wants you to drive her to the mall will know not to ask for this at 7 p.m. on Tuesday because the answer is going to be no. As one Tranquility by Tuesday participant wrote, "I've learned that once you claim a time, things just naturally shift around to accommodate it. So rather than trying to clear out everything else and then scheduling the activity, just claim that time first and everything else will shift."

Participant perspectives: Overcoming logistical challenges

Once you've decided to take one night for you, a few strategies can help you keep that commitment, even if you do have young kids or an intense work schedule (or both).

1. Cover for one another.

In two-parent families with young kids, the most practical approach to this rule is for each parent to cover the other's night off. Indeed, an explicit quid pro quo offer is probably the best way to get your other half on board with this idea.

"My partner and I agree that both of us should have our own night to do something fun—he takes Wednesday nights and goes cycling with his buddies and I take Thursdays for tae kwon do," one person reported. "We put these on the calendar and know not to schedule anything over them unless it's absolutely necessary. If we do need to schedule something during that time, we make sure we free up a different night for that person."

Another, whose partner sang in a choir on Mondays, noted that it was "helpful to have both of us have a weekly commitment. It helps us honor the other's schedule and keep each other accountable for doing something that makes our lives fuller and richer." A direct trade-off is not only fair, it's wise, because any long-term relationship is going to be more satisfying when both parties feel supported in becoming their best selves. Plus, everyone is going to be happier when both parties get a real break.

To be sure, not everyone lived in such a family, or had partners who were equally into this rule. One person whose partner was a "definite homebody" reported that their deal was to give each person a block of time; if the homebody wished to do solo projects around the house, so be it. (One way to get at the spirit of this rule is for the covering party to take the kids *out of the house* for the designated block, so the homebody can revel in the silence.)

2. Hire help.

Trading off is easiest, but if you have a partner with an intense or unpredictable work schedule, the next best option is to hire regular childcare for your night off, which is another reason to make a commitment. Most people won't go to the trouble of arranging this care to do something that can be done flexibly. Simply assume your partner will not be there, and make the appropriate arrangements.

A few study participants who considered this option spoke of guilt, though let's be clear: in a two-parent family, the default childcare split is fifty-fifty. If your partner is not available to do that, then an evening of childcare is not outsourcing *you*.

It is outsourcing *your partner*. If this person does not feel guilty about not being there, neither should you! Childcare costs money, but again, if work demands preclude your partner from sharing childcare with you, then I believe work should be adequately compensating your partner for this availability. I also believe that your sanity is then worth some of this compensation.

And if you are the partner with the unpredictable or intense work schedule? Encourage your partner to take a night for him or herself, and help arrange for coverage. Then figure out when you might be able to take a few hours too. If weekday evenings seem dicey, consider an early weekend-morning session. (If you have been traveling all week, do Sunday morning rather than Saturday, because your partner is definitely going to want you to cover Saturday morning—unless you arrange regular childcare for this spot as well.)

3. Find the predictable in the unpredictable.

I know that some jobs don't seem to lend themselves to during-the-week commitments. It's understood to be part of the bargain. But certain creative and collaborative approaches could change that.

I have long been intrigued by the "predictable time off" concept described in Leslie Perlow's book *Sleeping with Your Smartphone*. A consulting company implemented a policy where each team member got one planned-in-advance night off. No client coverage, no emails, no calls. On some level this seemed strange. Consultants are usually at their client sites Monday through Thursday, so what were they supposed to do, sit in the hotel room? But the program still had positive effects. People found gyms in their clients' cities where they could go to a regular Tuesday-night spinning class, or they made standing dates to call friends, or one could imagine finding anything from regular Tuesday-night performances to vespers services. All of these would make life feel far more sustainable than spending that evening in the inbox.

Perlow's idea—great as it is—hasn't taken off widely, but I'd note that the "unpredictable" aspect of some jobs might still be reasonably predictable. One Tranquility by Tuesday participant with a fluctuating shift schedule could not request the same night off every week (which would "incur the wrath of my colleagues"). However, this organization created the shift schedule two months in advance, so it was possible to look and see which night was most frequently free and find an activity or class for then. "I know I won't make every class, but that's OK," this person wrote. It was still worth trying.

4. Take advantage of community support.

Single parents face more challenges in taking a night off, as they do in general, but in this case, the sanity upside is even more critical. One evening (or a few Saturday hours) of childcare can be the difference between burnout and sustainability.

Absent that, swapping with a friend, neighbor, or relative can work, as can hunting for activities that support your situation. Some gyms have childcare. Some houses of worship do too, during events when parents would be there. It might also be possible to find something you enjoy during times when the children are occupied. You take an art class offered at the same time that your daughter has ballet. One budding tennis player wrote that "my son was already in a class at the same time an adult beginner class was offered, so I decided it wouldn't inconvenience anyone for me to sign up! I am usually already the one taking my son to that tennis lesson so instead of walking laps in the park or scrolling my phone during the lesson, I am learning something also!"

There are a million kid activities out there, so feel free to direct them toward ones that will offer you intriguing opportunities as well.

Participant perspectives: Overcoming emotional challenges

Beyond the practical challenges to implementing this rule, a few folks bristled at the idea of putting any more "stuff" in their lives. "I don't tend to enjoy regular commitments in my leisure time," one person wrote, with others not wanting "to add another thing."

I know it is fashionable to talk about how overcommitted

everyone already is and that we all need to be saying "no" more often. Sometimes this is true, but when people feel overcommitted, it is generally because their calendars are packed with lots of commitments that they *don't* want to do. I agree that you should clear your schedule of as many of these as you can. Perhaps you can't escape them by tomorrow, but with determination, you might wind down your involvement in six months.

I don't want anyone to feel drained or exhausted. With this rule, I am talking about commitments that really, truly excite you. You want to feel glowing, like Hannah after her weekly tennis game, or me after I've just mastered a tricky Poulenc melody. I'd like to think that in this great big world, and if you gave yourself six months to figure this out, you'd find *something*. Let your energy be your guide. If it makes you feel depleted, you're headed in the wrong direction. If you get more excited every time you think about your upcoming Tuesday commitment, you're on the right track.

In any case, most weekly commitments don't take huge quantities of time—a realization that can help counter worries about exhaustion. Hannah spends about an hour and a half per week on her tennis games. If you leave the house at 6:45 p.m. for a 7 p.m. rehearsal, and are home at 9:15 p.m., that is two and a half hours out of the week's 168.

Looking at the numbers might also help with the guilt that respondents worried about feeling when they dared to have interests beyond work and family.

One professor wrote that "I usually miss seeing my son two

nights a week when I have to work late and commute an hour from my farther campus. It results in not wanting to miss another night with him for 'me time' because I feel guilty about not spending time with him." However, this person wrote, "I know from time tracking that I do spend more time with him than most working moms get to spend with their kids, so I need to get over the mom-guilt" even as it was also possible to "set better boundaries around work."

I'd note that it is also possible to cut yourself some slack on other things in life. One person, in explaining why this rule might not work, recounted a weekly schedule of house chores: "Monday is the kitchen, Tuesday is laundry, Wednesday is the garage, etc. So if I take a night off, my schedule is off." I am still puzzled about what sort of disaster will ensue if the garage cleaning gets moved earlier in the evening or just doesn't happen. If you find yourself thinking this way, try to come up with an activity that you love so much that you wouldn't care about a little extra clutter in the garage.

I'm all about dispensing with unnecessary guilt, but as I explored the answers from those who were most adamant that this rule would never work, I came across something more pernicious than garden-variety self-reproach: **Some people are deeply invested in the idea that their families or workplaces would not function in their absence**.

This often gets framed as a lament that people have no time for themselves, but when you push for the reasons why, the real explanation becomes evident soon enough.

One Tranquility by Tuesday participant rued that "What is the point of taking a night for fun and getting home to a sink full of dirty dishes?" Others spoke of their partners being unable to handle bedtime for multiple small children. Or it was impossible to find responsible childcare.

In the workplace version, no assistant is qualified to speak for someone in their absence, colleagues can't be trusted to handle that client, and you just can't hire good employees these days.

It is true that no one is perfect, but fundamentally, all of this is arrogance in disguise—or fear, which is the flip side of the same coin. It is clinging to the idea that *only I can do the things I do. Without me, everything will fall apart.* The fear-based version is that *if I allow for the possibility that things won't fall apart, then what is the point of me?*

The point of all of us is that human beings have inherent worth, apart from anything we do. This is fortunate, because the idea that everything will fall apart without us is almost universally false. We all have things we do uniquely well, and yet the world will go on spinning in all of our absences. If they had to, our families, colleagues, and friends would all figure something out.

This is certainly true for run-of-the-mill situations. Children would eventually sleep. The dirty dishes would get cleaned or people would eat on paper plates. Colleagues would figure out what you do or they'd do something else.

I believe it also needs to be true in more challenging situations. A few Tranquility by Tuesday participants were caring for family members with complex medical conditions. Continuous care very much matters—and yet it's also a matter of safety that another person's well-being not depend, entirely, on somebody who can get ill or worse. If your extended family and community would figure something out if you were gone completely . . . then perhaps you can come up with a solution that would allow for a two-hour respite on a Tuesday night.

Being willing to let go of this narrative that *no one can function without me* is liberating. For starters, you can explore enjoyable pastimes that require commitment and presence, which is the simple point of this rule. The larger point is realizing that other people can augment one's capabilities substantially. Your partner will do things differently, and that's great. Your employees will come up with amazing ideas. Your community can support you when you are facing challenging life situations. When we don't need to micromanage every minute, life feels a lot more tranquil. This is worth challenging some narratives for.

The results

Over the years, taking one night for you can change the experience of time. One participant said on the survey that this rule had been a family tradition since a now-teenaged child had been six months old. Each parent got either Monday and Wednesday or Tuesday and Thursday "off" after dinner. "Once the kitchen was cleaned up, one parent did the baby evening routine while the other parent went to wander the library stacks for an hour, or hit golf balls at the range, went to a coffee shop, for a bike ride, etc. Just for an hour and a half or so—but it was a game changer in our early parenting days."

Participants who tried taking a night off made time for all sorts of fun. One person spent several evening hours photographing the spring blossoms. One devoted an evening to creative writing. Interestingly, several got ideas for bigger commitments simply from taking the night off once. "I went to coffee with a friend. It was nice having an adult conversation!" one person wrote. "We decided to start a regular book club together." Another person who took two hours to play music decided to sign up for a course.

Several people modified the rule—taking an intentionally long lunch break once a week, for instance, because there was already regular childcare coverage—but in any case, simply having this time changed people's perspective. "I often feel like everyone else is in control of my time and this helped me feel like I had a little say in how I spend my time," one person wrote. "I'm also hoping it can become a standing date that I can look forward to throughout the week."

This anticipation by itself lifted people's moods. "I felt a sense of expansiveness and relaxation that carried over for a few days," one person wrote, with another noting that "I only took an hour, but it felt nice to make plans just for me—to go to a local park, catch up with a friend, and get some light exercise. I felt refreshed when I got home."

Taking a few hours just for ourselves reminds us that we can exercise control over our schedules. "I'm seeing the benefits of planning more things for myself," one person wrote. "I think previously I was relying on other people to bring opportunities to me, and it's a big mood lifter to take control and build some fun things into my monthly calendar for myself." We are reminded of our own sense of agency when we are able to feel like "life is more than work and home and taking care of everything," as one person put it. Or as another noted, "I feel more like me when I'm doing something I enjoy and am responsible only for myself. It's fun to see progress on my hobbies."

This sense of progress is one of the best reasons to make fun into a commitment. There is a deep joy that comes from learning a difficult piece of music over several weeks, and having its demanding beauty seep into your brain. A regular art class results in a handful of finally completed paintings. You experience the rush of performing a play with that community drama troupe. Your softball team wins the championship. What could be more fun than that?

The benefits outweigh the challenges

I know that this rule is not easy. I know that it requires people to challenge assumptions. I have been teaching this rule for long enough that I know it is a hard sell. In the one-month follow-up after the Tranquility by Tuesday study, respondents listed this as the most difficult rule to implement. But there was evidence that its benefits were accruing over time. I asked people in the course of the survey about whether they regularly had time "just for me." A promising 64 percent of people reported taking a night off from work and family responsibilities during the week they learned this rule. By the one-month follow-up, 12 percent more people agreed that they regularly had time for themselves, as compared with before they began the Tranquility by Tuesday project.

Building in time just for you takes time to make happen. It is also worth the time.

As we devote regular time to things we love, we discover the truth that time is elastic. It will stretch to accommodate what we truly wish to put into it. And so, we don't build the lives we want by saving time here and there. Instead, when we build the lives we want, with space for what feels life-giving, we discover that time can hold a lot more than we might have thought.

I certainly saw this when I interviewed Kathleen Paley for the "Best of Both Worlds" podcast. This lawyer at a major D.C. law firm and mother of two had at one point felt exhausted with all her responsibilities—that dark time many people go through when it feels like "work and family is taking up everything," she told me on the podcast, and "every bit of you, as an individual, has to be put on the back burner for a while." But, she noted, "that's not sustainable in the long term."

Instead of dialing down the career that she loved, or phoning it in at home, Kathleen elected to focus on her energy. "A lot of the time when we feel tired, it's not necessarily that our bodies are lacking energy," she told me. "It's that our minds need change."

So she went on the attack against exhaustion by pursuing her long-time interest in local development and economic growth. She began volunteering with the Fairfax City Economic Development Authority, and then scaled up this commitment over time. She made the space by examining the rest of her hours. For instance, she and her husband used to watch an hour of TV most nights after the kids went to bed. Even though it was only an hour, she realized that the energy-sapping nature of passive screen time meant that somehow she wasn't getting anything else done on those nights. So they cut the TV slot down to two nights a week. In this newly freed-up space, she found that she could do all manner of other, energizing things, including working on her town's small business incubator, and helping organize Restaurant Week. Eventually, she was voted in as the development authority's new chairperson, which was a role that would allow her to make an even bigger difference in her city. "It's wonderful to see this place you live in become more robust and exciting," she said.

When you take one night for you, it often doesn't just benefit you. That's true for people like Kathleen, who use the time to volunteer, but it's also true for folks whose night off is more personal in nature. When we renew our spirits, we have more energy for all our responsibilities. We can be more tranquil about life when we know our spirits will be fed.

Take the next step

◆

TAKE A DAY FOR YOU

Taking one night for you is about making a commitment to something other than work or family responsibilities. Once you've established that both can function in your absence, it's time to try something a little more challenging: taking a whole day for you.

I don't mean an all-day golfing extravaganza or day at the spa, though if that would make you happy, that's worth building into the schedule. I mean taking a day to ask yourself big questions about what you want your life to look like.

Joan Dunlop, a pediatric allergist and immunologist, has built her career in a nontraditional way, choosing to go back to do her medical subspecialty training after spending nine years mostly caring for her three children. As she's made these big career decisions, she's taken personal mini-retreats to ponder how she's spending her time, and what she'd like her time to look like. Sometimes this has been a half day in a coffee shop, but sometimes it's a day at a local hotel. She looks at five spheres of life: her marriage, her spiritual health, her children, her work, and her physical health. She lists what she's doing in each area, what stage of life she's currently in, and what changes she'd like to make.

Her personal retreat days have given her space to think about how she can be strategic. For instance, during her early years of motherhood, Joan was working one day a week in an emergency room to keep her hand in medicine. As her kids got older, she realized that she might be able to give work a little more mental space. Since she was working part-time, the most obvious way to scale up would be to go full-time. However, she realized that in an emergency-room setting, more hours would mean more similar hours, which wasn't the sort of expansion she was desiring. So she decided, instead, to use her expanding mental space to train as an allergist and immunologist—a speciality she was seeing a lot with one of her own children—and after many years is now working in an academic medical center advancing research in this field.

Joan suggests these days apart for anyone. "It keeps you from just doing the next thing because it's in front of you," she says. "If you don't take time to plan or think about or evaluate how you're spending your time, you won't suddenly wake up one day doing nothing. You'll be doing what everyone around you is doing." If you're a lawyer, you'll be gunning for partner. If you're a stay-at-home parent, you'll take on a leadership role in the PTA. But is that the right step? Is that what you want to do? A day apart can help you figure this out.

Plus, notes Joan, these days "ideally keep me from being too angsty in the day-to-day. Writing project not going well? My mind immediately jumps to: Maybe I shouldn't be trying to 'make it' in such a big career. Child makes off-handed comment about wanting me to attend something I can't make it to? I second-guess my priorities." But when she knows she has a day apart to think about her time regularly, she can push these concerns aside in the moment, knowing that she will think about her overall time allotments later on.

If a night off is challenging, a day off could be even harder. But it still might be possible. Maybe you can make use of a friend's house while he's traveling. If a full day seems impossible, try a half day. Instead of going to work in the morning, you take a personal day and go somewhere else for a few hours: a park in nice weather, a library. Think ahead of time about what questions you might like to ask yourself. Plan out your time so you can use it wisely. I'm not promising you'll have any huge breakthroughs. But it's hard to think big when we're caught up in day-to-day logistics. A day apart creates space. And sometimes, that is all we really need.

Your turn

───────────◆───────────

TAKE ONE NIGHT FOR YOU

Planning questions:

1. Do you have any recurring fun-for-you commitments outside of work and family? (Examples might include a book club, choir rehearsals, or a weekly golf game.)

2. If you don't already have a weekly fun-for-you commitment, what would you do with one night off (or an equivalent amount of weekend time) per week? If you already take time for a fun-for-you commitment, is there an additional activity you'd like to add so that you have something fun-for-you on the calendar every week?

3. If you are not currently taking a night just for you, what would you need to do to make this happen? If you are

currently doing this, how have you created space in
your life?

4. What might prevent you from taking one night off?

5. How can you address these challenges?

Implementation questions:

1. Did you take a few hours off from work and family
responsibilities this week? What did you do with
this time?

2. If you didn't take one night (or another block of time) just for
you during the past week, do you have an idea for what you
might do with a night off in upcoming weeks?

3. What effects did you see from taking one night (or at least a
few hours) for your interests?

4. What challenges did you face while trying to take some time
for your interests?

5. How did you address these challenges?

6. Did you modify this strategy? If so, how?

7. How likely are you to continue using this rule in your life?

PART 3

◆

Waste Less Time

Habits for creating more restorative space

*H*as this ever happened to you? You show up at work, ready to spend the morning completing a top-priority task. But first you need to take care of a little paperwork, and then there's a flurry of emails about another project and, next thing you know, it's time for that 10:30 meeting.

Or perhaps you have a weekend hour or two before anyone needs to be anywhere. The kids are all quiet, and you go upstairs to grab your book, but first you remember that you need to order batteries, so you pick up your phone to do that, and take a quick look at your news alerts, and suddenly it is only ten minutes until you need to be in the car.

It is so easy to waste time, though I want to clarify what I mean by that phrase. I saw a sign in an Airbnb house I'd rented for a weekend recently assuring visitors that "Time you enjoyed wasting isn't wasted time." The illustration evoked little clouds. The message—appropriate for a farmhouse in a valley ringed by fall-colorful mountains—was that staring at the sky is a perfectly lovely way to pass the hours, and I agree. Letting your mind wander from a swaying hammock can restore serenity, which is a highly productive enterprise. Time spent on something you find meaningful isn't wasted either, even if the outcome isn't exactly what you wished.

Instead, I define wasted time as when we spend minutes, hours, even days mindlessly on things we don't care about. And by that definition, many of us waste unfortunate amounts of time on things that don't look at all like staring at the clouds. We chop up what could be an hour of focused creative time by answering an email that could have waited. Or we fritter away what could have been twenty minutes lying in a hammock reading the responses to the comment a middle-school acquaintance posted on someone else's breakfast photo. Our lives will end someday and here we are, letting time circle down the drain, doing things that don't matter at all.

It is easy to spend time mindlessly, but we do not have to just let these waters swirl. These final two Tranquility by Tuesday rules are about how to waste less time on things that do not deserve nearly as much time as we give them. While it is far more important to fill life with the good stuff first, by compressing the space available for the small tasks of life, we can create more of a sense of time abundance. By changing the mindless habits of leisure time, we can spend this time in more enjoyable ways. We might even start to feel like we have more free time than we thought we did. Feeling like we have more free time can completely change the stories we tell ourselves about our lives.

Even with these shifts, it is impossible to spend time perfectly. Everybody wastes time. I certainly waste time. It is the human condition. Perfection is not the goal. Progress is, and every minute spent more enjoyably, or more meaningfully, is a little victory. These final two rules can make those victories happen.

RULE 8

Batch the Little Things

Tasks expand to fill the available space. When we give them less time, they take less time.

Some five hundred pages into *War and Peace*, one of Tolstoy's main characters, Prince Andrei, encounters a rather time-less problem. This cerebral aristocrat has big ideas for reforming the Russian military. He comes to Petersburg to share them. He soon finds himself on an important committee that is, theoretically, an honor. But as he goes from appointment to appointment, he finds that, "the mechanics of life, the arrangement of the day so as to be on time everywhere, absorbed the greater part of his vital energy," Tolstoy writes. Indeed, "he was so busy for whole days together that he had no time to think about the fact that he was doing nothing."

I underlined this passage as soon as I read it because, well, who can't sympathize? Sometimes it feels like whole weeks can disappear into a general frenzy of stuff that must be done. Signing and scanning forms. Checking on logistics. Scheduling meetings, and then rescheduling them when something else comes up and the battle plan needs to change. Evenings and weekends can likewise disappear into chores, errands, and the preparation of one day for another. All this activity means that we feel incredibly busy. No one is loafing around. Yet it is hard to understand, at the end of a particular day, what progress has been achieved. Not for Andrei's military, and perhaps not for our personal or professional goals either.

All the administrative and maintenance tasks of life feel like they eat up hours. But the most curious part of this is that, at least according to time diaries, much of the stuff we busy ourselves with does not actually take much time. A few calls, a few forms, a few responses. We often spend more time going over these tasks in our minds—agonizing over their existence and expanding their mental real estate—than actually doing them.

The bigger problem with such schedule clutter is that even if these tasks are annoying, they don't take much effort, and, once finished, they provide the satisfaction of being obviously "done." Many of the important things in life, such as nurturing our family relationships, or advancing in our careers, are not so obviously "done." They deserve time, and lots of it, but the rewards are not so immediately obvious as checking something off a list.

And so, insidiously, the lure of easy accomplishment with the little tasks can chop up the day and make people feel like they are making progress, even though, when it comes to what matters, they are not.

The solution is **Tranquility by Tuesday Rule 8: Batch the little things**. Designate a small chunk of time to tackle those things that must be done, but aren't your top priorities. This could be an afternoon half-hour during the workday, or a bigger blast on Fridays, or a ninety-minute chore, errand, or personal task blitz on one weekend day. When a small task occurs to you or pops up in your inbox, don't just do it. Put it on the list for your batch processing time, and tackle all of these small tasks then.

This rule to batch the little things has two important effects.

1. It forces prioritization.

If you give yourself one hour to get up to speed on the little tasks lingering in your inbox, you will not deliberate over an unimportant response. If you have a small window to buy a birthday present, schedule a haircut, and fill out the required forms for your kid's school, you will not search through the entire universe of birthday-present options. If you have an hour to pick up the house on Saturdays, you will focus on actions with the biggest impact. Tasks expand to fill the available space. When we give them less time, they take less time.

2. It keeps little tasks from always being an option.

You know that there is a specific time to order that present, sign that form, and call your dentist. It is hard enough to build "deep work" into a schedule, or time to focus on relationships or time to rejuvenate. You don't want to interrupt yourself... or at least you *shouldn't* want to interrupt yourself. If you find yourself feeling bad about a dirty floor at some point other than your Saturday window, you can remind yourself that there is a time for cleaning up, and now is not that time. You don't need to feel guilty that you aren't doing a particular task. You can let yourself relax. By batching the little things, we can leave other swathes of time open for more meaningful work, or fun.

This rule sounds simple, but it is hard to follow, mostly because it goes against some ingrained notions of what it means to be productive. Crossing little things off the list feels productive, whereas spending long chunks of time wrestling with complex matters does not. But there is no substitute for time and attention. The question is just what we give our time and attention to.

How to batch the little things: Six steps

After introducing this rule to the Tranquility by Tuesday participants, I asked them to follow a six-step process for building this new habit into their lives.

1. Learn to identify small tasks.

I asked people to think back over the last twenty-four hours. What small, nonurgent tasks made it onto their daily to-do lists? What about small tasks that they completed as soon as they thought about them, even if they were doing something else at the time? Common answers included signing a kid up for something, mailing a package, paying a bill, responding to invitations, returning objects to their homes, purchasing household items, making routine appointments, sending requested information, and so forth. There's no need to make a comprehensive list of all the little tasks in your life—their nature makes that hard—but learning how to identify these not-terribly-important items makes batching them possible. Pay attention for a day or two and you'll start to recognize them.

2. Determine how much time you need.

I asked people to estimate how much time they devoted to small tasks over the past seven days, both professionally and personally (I did not have people include ongoing household chores such as food preparation and laundry in this calculation; these can be batched if you'd like, but the process will look a little different). People's guesses centered around two hours a week, with a general range of one to four hours, though one put-upon respondent claimed a number that amounted to every waking minute.

My sense is that for most people, one to four hours per week is about right, with those managing complex households or with less administrative support at work coming in toward the top of the range, and those with simpler lives coming in at the bottom. While this range of time isn't nothing—I'm sure many of us would love one to four more hours per week to read or do hobbies—it's also not exactly the 24/7 time frame it can sometimes feel like.

This is an important point, even if there are major social questions about who carries what proportion of any given household's mental load. Likewise, plenty of workplaces under-invest in support staff and then expect people to pick up the slack along predictably stereotypical lines. These questions are worth addressing in any situation that feels inequitable. However, there are also things we can do personally to lighten whatever proportion of the load we happen to be carrying. A key realization here is that these **tasks often feel bigger than they are because they can constantly weigh on us if we're not careful**. You can spend your life remembering that you need to book the dog sitter for an upcoming trip and switch the carpool for the week you have that conference. That is true even though each might involve a thirty-second text or email.

3. Identify times, and where you might get stuck.

I asked people to think about when they could schedule a time during the workday to tackle small tasks (including personal tasks that have to happen during business hours). I also asked about a weekly chore window for home tasks (with perhaps a small daily window for the daily tasks). When could people make this happen—and what might prevent this batching?

People anticipated various challenges. For instance, some work is, by nature, more reactive than other work.

"When there is a deadline that comes up unexpectedly it doesn't matter if I have time scheduled at the end of the day if my boss needs an answer immediately," one person wrote. "For example, I just had to drop everything to find stats for a news article that came up regarding an event I am running. The deadline for the paper was in three hours. I can't just say 'oh well, my batch time is scheduled for 4:30 p.m. so I'll get to it then.'"

This may be true, although I'd argue that we can still distinguish the urgent from the nonurgent. Even people who do traffic in tight deadlines often have other sorts of work—like filling out that random form from HR—that can be batched. It might help to analyze a few days' or a week's worth of tasks and sort them into what can wait and what can't. The goal is to make both sorts of tasks feel less frenzied by separating them out.

A few people worried that the little things would seek them out, even if they tried to ignore them until batching time. One person, who anticipated this problem, pledged to "put the phone on Do Not Disturb and turn off the audio 'ding' that alerts me to a new email when I'm working on something else." Another person decided to stop all notifications, and chose a few times per day to scan emails and messages without actually opening them, to ensure there was nothing time-sensitive.

Some people feared that small tasks would nag at them. "My brain works better if I get the excess thoughts out of it," one person explained. People mentioning this challenge did these small tasks immediately either because they worried they would forget them, or would remember them at 3 a.m., or wouldn't be able to compartmentalize the tasks and would think about them constantly until they got done.

4. Start writing things down.

As I looked through the Tranquility by Tuesday survey responses, I realized that many people who worried about forgetting tasks, or who worried that they would constantly think of undone tasks, had no actual list of tasks to be done other than, as one person put it, "the running one in my head." Some people who managed to keep work lists lost this skill when it came to their personal lives, which resulted in frenetically tackling tasks as soon as they came up.

If this sounds like you, it's time to build a new habit. The human brain is a terrible place to keep lists. When a task occurs to you, write it down somewhere you know you will look: a planner, your calendar, even an email to yourself (if you process emails into doable task lists). I keep a running Friday "punch list" on my weekly planner page, which I address at some point during this generally-pretty-open day. My friend Lisa Woodruff, owner of the Organize 365 company, teaches people to keep what she calls a "Sunday Basket." All small tasks get tossed, physically, in this basket—from library books to permission slips, to little scraps of paper with notes to yourself. The Sunday Basket then gets emptied and addressed during a batch processing time on Sunday.

Corralling or listing tasks will keep you from forgetting the tasks, and once you designate a batch time, you will probably stop worrying about any given task until that time. You know there will be a time to address it. Now is not that time. What would have been a "nagging task" becomes much like that dentist appointment that you've scheduled for next Wednesday morning at 8 a.m. Most of us don't obsess about that dentist appointment, hour after hour, because it is "undone." It is a defined task, for a designated time, so our brains are good. The same thing happens when you commit to filling out that form at 1:30 p.m. on Friday.

Writing things down doesn't solve all to-do list anxiety, but it does reduce it a great deal. In a busy life, a little reduction in anxiety can make a big difference.

"I tried to keep a little post-it note list near me, so anytime I thought of a little thing I would normally have stopped to do, I just wrote it down and trusted that it would get done later during 'batch' time," one person wrote, noting that this helped limit distractions and the sense of being constantly behind.

5. Match the right work to the right time.

A few people worried that I was suggesting carving out a big chunk of prime time for all these little things, which inspired resistance along these lines: "Large blocks of time on my calendar during the week are an extreme luxury, and I use them for deep work. I keep a list of one-offs to check off in the inevitable five minutes I end up with between work meetings."

I agree that if you have only one two-hour chunk of time during your workweek, you should not give this over to batching the little things. You should also not batch process during your most productive hours. I call this bad habit "clearing the decks," a phrase from Tolstoy's time that involved securing and putting away everything on a ship's decks before battle.

While clearing the decks might be wise in naval warfare, it is counterproductive in daily life. What happens is that people start the workday with grand intentions and a long to-do list. Most of the items are little. A few are big. It is tempting to batch process all the little ones first, so your mind is theoretically clear to focus on the big stuff later. But this rarely works in practice because everyone runs out of steam. The little things get finished by mid-morning, you go to a meeting, you cycle through an email check and reading headlines, it's time for lunch, your energy crashes, and tackling the big things no longer feels possible. Far better to find a thirty- to sixty-minute chunk during a non-peak period for most of the little things, and use that early-morning energy for the day's most important tasks. As for those few minutes between meetings? They might be better used to decompress, think about the next meeting, chat with a colleague, or read.

6. Find a way to make it work.

Perhaps the ideal would be to shove everything nonurgent to Friday, but in practice, other people will try to make the nonurgent urgent, and sometimes shifting gears does feel nice. The good news is that the perfect doesn't need to be the enemy of the good. The chosen batch processing time doesn't need to be long or even all-encompassing if you plan to do multiple batching sessions. Any ten- to sixty-minute window where you tackle more than one small task can likely keep with this rule. It's constantly flitting in and out of what should be focused time (or dedicated relaxation time) that is the problem. *That's* the bad habit that can keep you from doing anything else.

The productivity trap

Turning off notifications and making a list is simple enough. The bigger problem for many Tranquility by Tuesday participants was that this rule to batch the little things—both at work and at home—interfered with some ingrained notions of what productivity looks like:

- "I like the idea of batching household chores. But I also feel like I have a 'I have too much on my plate' mindset right now that makes me feel irresponsible if I'm not constantly taking care of something."
- "Life right now is more about getting things done when you can because you can't rely on any given time slot being protected."

We like to get stuff done. This is true of humanity in general. As for the subset of humanity that reads time-management and productivity books? We *really* like to cross stuff off the list. The physical act of crossing something off provides an incredible sense of satisfaction. Indeed, I have been known to write things on my to-do list after doing them just so I can cross them off. We walk around with the maxims in our heads to not put off until tomorrow what can be done today and to make hay while the sun shines. A number of Tranquility by Tuesday participants cited the "two-minute rule," which comes up in a lot of productivity literature. The idea is that if a task will take two minutes (or less time), you should just do it when you learn of it, so you won't have to deal with it again.

On some level, the two-minute rule makes sense. It might take more than two minutes to pull that task up a second time and get in the mental space to address it. But there are complications with the two-minute rule that ultimately undermine its benefits. Any two-minute task can easily turn into one of these three monsters:

1. A Task Hydra

Are you *sure* that's only a simple two-minute task? Few people excel at time estimation. That two-minute task can easily turn into a five- or ten-minute task, or a multipart task that involves waiting for someone to call you back, or finding that you need to track down a different form, or print something when you don't have a printer nearby. One person referred to this phenomenon as the "Task Hydra." Cut off one head and the task grows another. Soon enough you've really cut into the time when you intended to do something else.

2. A Rabbit Hole

It is hard to resume work after a distraction. Yes, it takes only a minute to email your colleague that form she asked you for. But after you send that email you find yourself, shockingly enough, *in your inbox.* Your inbox turns out to have lots of other shiny new unread messages. You start opening them and reading them and . . . two minutes turns into twenty. And that's if you stay in your inbox. Some folks have elaborate rituals that precede the resumption of work. Any break results in checking headlines, the stock market, sports scores, two social-media apps, and the weather. Focus becomes the exception, rather than the rule.

3. A Procrastination Siren

The biggest problem is that the two-minute rule (or even a five- or ten-minute rule) can be an easy way to procrastinate doing the more difficult stuff, a phenomenon the most self-aware participants quickly figured out:

- "When I'm at my computer, I often take care of personal things—ordering presents, looking up a bike route, etc.—because it's easier and more fun than work."
- "I want to feel productive and small tasks make it easy to feel like I've completed a lot of things, even if they have distracted me from a larger, more important task."
- "I sometimes have a hard time motivating myself for doing anything productive at all, so these small tasks come in handy."
- "When I feel frustrated it's nice to have something to 'mark off.' Sometimes there is value in that, but often I need to sit and really dig into the hard things."

The "Task Hydra" and the "Rabbit Hole" phenomena can eat up time, but ultimately this last monster is the most dangerous. Sometimes you just need to sit and stare at a screen, or a notebook, or the piano keys or a canvas if you're pondering a composition.

You need to sit with the discomfort as your brain works to figure out what you need to do. When you give yourself an easy win, you deprive yourself of the bigger win that comes from breaking through. And while, yes, you do need breaks, you're probably better off disconnecting completely than answering emails.

"If my brain feels stumped, I'd like to stand up and stretch or go for a walk—something that still allows a part of my brain to work on the problem," one person wrote. As you go for a walk, your brain slowly knits disparate strands together. You come back refreshed and with an answer. In the grand scheme of things, this feels better than crossing six meaningless items off a to-do list.

The three-hour rule

If the "two-minute rule" isn't all it's cracked up to be, then what? A few years ago, one of my wise blog readers shared what she called "the three-hour rule," which gave her a way to get both the big and little stuff done.

Each day, she would spend a few minutes looking at email and planning out her workflow, and then, from 9 a.m. to noon she would go silent. She would turn off all notifications, shut her inbox, turn off her phone, and focus completely on her big problem of the day. She would emerge to the world at lunchtime and spend the rest of the day on calls, meetings, administrative work, and so forth. By following the "three-hour rule," she still completed all her two-minute tasks. But she also made progress on her major projects.

I know that all work is not the same. Plenty of careers, from medicine to construction to retail, don't fit this mold. Even those in knowledge-work occupations may already be coming up with reasons why the three-hour rule would never work. And maybe it wouldn't. But if we allowed for calls from the school nurse, daycare, or your spouse, would that change your mind? What if you had an honest conversation with your manager or your direct reports about preserving time for focus—for everyone? Have you ever been unreachable during a three-hour flight? Or even just a ninety-minute one? Did the earth stop spinning?

To change your daily life, change your narrative

Sometimes, we become addicted to the notion of being busy, and that we constantly have to do one thing or another. *I have no time for thinking about my next career move because I have to respond to all these meeting requests! I can't meet up with a friend or write that book proposal because I have to buy light bulbs and mail that package and . . .* Consciously pushing these tasks into a smaller window means there might be time for other things. This sounds great, but acknowledging that there is time for other things might mean changing a narrative. And changing a narrative is hard. Changing a narrative can require changing an identity. *I am no longer the put-upon martyr, doing everything for everyone else. I'm a person who could be having fun, or could be making progress on my professional goals, but because of my choices, is not.*

Ultimately, there are no prizes given for enjoying your life the least. And there are no prizes given for being too busy to get what matters done. If you like how you spend your time, great. If you don't like it, change it. Batching the little things is one way to gather back time from that sense of having your vital energy drained away by life's mundanities—and to preserve that energy for what is most important to you.

The results

It was with this goal in mind that the Tranquility by Tuesday participants tried this rule out for a week—creating little windows for the little things, so they could keep big chunks of time for the big things. Most people chose an afternoon block during the workday for their batch processing, which is a great time. It's when most people's energy dips, and those easy wins can be motivating. Many followed my lead in creating a bigger batching window on Fridays for the things that tended to stack up. Doing so had all sorts of positive effects.

Most notably, people made progress on their priorities when

they weren't constantly interrupting themselves. "I felt like I did get more work done during the morning hours this week," one person who batched the little things in the afternoon wrote. Another reported that this rule improved focus because "it felt like I was scheduling the to-dos instead of being interrupted by them."

"Knowing there's a time to get to those little things has helped me prioritize the important but nonurgent things during the workday," one person wrote, with another enjoying being able to "say to myself, there is a time designated for that, and it's not now." A quarter more people agreed that they had had time for what they wanted to do during Week 8 of the Tranquility by Tuesday project than reported that they had had enough time "yesterday" on the pre-program survey.

In addition to feeling like they had enough time, people felt better about the time they had. One respondent wrote of feeling "less frazzled." Another reported a "sense of accomplishment from 'all' being done that I usually don't feel when [the little tasks] are spread out through the week."

I was happiest to see enthusiasm from people who'd doubted whether this rule could work. One reluctant convert noted that, over the years, she had prided herself on her ability to squeeze things into the nooks and crannies of her schedule. But after trying this rule, she realized that always looking for a chance to tackle a small task "means I am always thinking about those little tasks," she wrote. "Blocking the effort is more efficient and less draining."

Over time, batching the little things can flip the entire narrative of how we approach our workdays. We're no longer squeezing in the good stuff amid everything else. We're doing what energizes us first, and confining the little things to the time we choose to give them. In a distracted world, this can be a real competitive advantage.

"I often feel overwhelmed by work email, as if everyone is asking something from me," one person wrote. After trying this rule, the person realized that "this impression came from the fact that I checked it every hour, so it 'felt' like I was nagged all the time." She decided that she would no longer allow herself to feel nagged. "Now with the batching around 3 p.m., I see the whole picture at once, I can process most of them, and decide when to do the few that really need more time before answering. I think I save time but mostly I think I change how I feel about work."

This can be true in our personal lives as well. One person who created a chore window on the weekend reported feeling "lower resentment for chores stealing my free time." In the newly open space, she pondered what she would really like to do. The answer? She spent most evenings outside after dinner or after daycare, taking in the longer days and warmer temperatures of spring. Time feels lighter when you don't constantly think you should be doing something else.

Take the next step

◆

LET GO OF SOMETHING

We can minimize by batching the little things, but the ultimate in minimizing is going to zero. There are a great many tasks in this world that do not need to be done.

This is one reason I suggest people track their time. When you know where the time goes, you can ask yourself why you are doing whatever it is you are doing. Maybe there's a good reason, but maybe there isn't. If that is the case, you can free up all sorts of space by exploring alternative ways of going through daily life.

For instance, you do not have to answer all emails. You definitely don't have to file or archive them. You can figure out if any given meeting really needs to happen, or if it could just be an email. Maybe you've been writing up a weekly report of something that you suspect doesn't get read. You could try not sending it and seeing what happens. If no one notices, that's a sign that it might not be critical.

You can take the same approach in your personal life. I don't meal plan. We have yet to starve. There are weeks when I don't put my laundry away. It sits in the basket until I need it again. My car gets rained on from time to time, which strikes me as a close approximation to washing it.

I know there are different schools of thought on this. I've watched Admiral William H. McRaven's famous "Make your bed" commencement speech like everyone else. I certainly aim to be conscientious about anything that deserves it. But I don't think that how we handle the little things is inevitably how we approach the bigger things. Time is limited. If you spend lots of time on the little things you risk running out of space for the bigger things. This doesn't mean we should be careless. It just means that time spent on one thing is time not spent on something else.

So if you do spend time on something, make sure you have a good reason. If not, ask what would happen if you didn't do it. Will chaos ensue? My bet is that nothing much will change—except you'll have more time than you would have by letting a little thing go.

Your turn

◆

BATCH THE LITTLE THINGS

Planning questions:

1. Think back over the past twenty-four hours. What "small tasks" have made it onto your daily to-do list? What about "small tasks" that you completed as soon as you thought about them, even if you were working on something else at the time?

2. How much time, in minutes, do you estimate you spent on these tasks last week?

3. When could you schedule a time at work each day, or each week, to tackle the small work tasks (and any personal tasks that have to happen during business hours)?

4. When could you schedule a weekly chore window—perhaps on the weekend or in the evening—to tackle small personal tasks?

5. What might prevent you from batching the little tasks in your life?

6. How could you deal with these challenges?

Implementation questions:

1. Think back over the past week. What times did you designate for little tasks during your workdays?

2. What windows did you designate for household tasks and chores?

3. What effect did you see in your life from batching the little things?

4. What challenges did you face in trying to batch the little things?

5. How did you address these challenges?

6. If you modified this rule, how did you do so?

7. How likely are you to continue using this rule in your life?

Effortful Before Effortless

Leisure time is too precious to be totally leisurely about leisure.

Jeremy Anderberg reads a lot. With a full-time job and three young children, he still manages to make it through about a hundred books a year. Over the past few years, he has read at least one biography of every U.S. president, and *War and Peace* (twice).

Perhaps this sounds like Jeremy spends every free minute reading. But he doesn't. He uses social media. He watches some TV, perhaps averaging about an hour a day of decidedly non–*War and Peace* fare, such as *The Bachelorette* or real-estate reality shows.

But because he loves to read—always feeling much more

emotionally and intellectually satisfied afterward than if he had mindlessly scrolled around online—he has structured his limited discretionary time to make reading happen *first*. He and his wife wake up around 5:45 a.m. most days and spend an hour reading in bed before the kids wake up. They read for thirty minutes or so before bed as well. And then, Jeremy looks for pockets in the day—the time that author Brigid Schulte once christened "time confetti"—when he might read for a few minutes. "When I'm waiting for something, or need a little break, if I always have a book available, then there's less choice in the matter, and less decision making needed," he says.

These chunks of time confetti add up. Jeremy estimates that they give him another 30 minutes or so of reading time per day. He can read about 50 pages per hour. Two hours of reading time per day comes out to 100 pages. That's 700 pages per week. That's usually about two 350-page books per week, which averages out to 100 books a year.

Now to be sure, it's not quite that simple. Figuring out what to read next, so each day's hundred pages proceed apace, takes time too. But on the whole, I think Jeremy's approach to leisure time is the right one, particularly for people who have busy lives and a lot of responsibilities.

Time-diary studies find that even the busiest people have *some* leisure time. The problem for most of us is that while some of this time is predictable (for instance, at night, or during weekend baby naps) it tends to happen at times when people don't exactly have the energy to climb mountains. As for the rest of this leisure, it tends to happen in patches of time that are unexpected, or short in duration, or might be easily interrupted.

Social media and screen time in general solve the problem of these constraints incredibly well. You don't need to plan to enjoy either option. You don't need a babysitter to watch TV at night while the kids are in bed, nor the mental bandwidth to do anything beyond settle into the couch cushions. You likely have your phone with you when time confetti appears, and scrolling can occupy anywhere from two minutes to two hours. That's why this "effortless" fun occupies the bulk of people's leisure time. Among U.S. social-media users, the average time spent on Facebook is 33 minutes per day, with 31 minutes spent on Twitter, and 29 minutes spent on Instagram. Any suddenly popular new addition (Snapchat, TikTok, Clubhouse . . .) cannibalizes some minutes from existing services but also takes up more time. As for old-fashioned television, according to the American Time Use Survey, in 2020, the average person with a full-time job still managed to watch 2.24 hours per day as a primary activity. Time is absolutely limited to twenty-four hours per day, and so this effortless leisure tends to crowd out time for more effortful fun such as reading, creative hobbies, or socializing with friends and family—things people claim they'd love to fit into their schedules, if only they could find the time.

The solution is **Tranquility by Tuesday Rule 9: Effortful before effortless**. Do just a few minutes of "effortful" fun before checking social media or turning on the TV. You can do this during any long patch of leisure, and as Jeremy does, during your time confetti too.

The upside of this rule is that when you do effortful fun *before* effortless fun, you get to do both. I'm not telling people to stop watching TV or to get off social media. I know there is a lot of excellent programming available these days. I also don't think that there is anything inherently more noble about reading a magazine write-up on low-calorie snacks versus watching a well-scripted drama (or looking at pretty outfits on Instagram). But if your kids go to bed or you finish with work or chores around 8 p.m., and you go to bed around 10:30 p.m., that's plenty of time to work on a puzzle for thirty minutes and *then* watch several TV shows. But if you turn on the TV first, it will feel hard to turn the TV off and muster the effort to start a puzzle, even if you really love doing puzzles, and even if sorting through a box for edge pieces is a more restorative brain break than watching two reality-show characters conspire to undermine a third. Same with the time confetti. It's hard to stop scrolling through Twitter to go read a poem. So you'll get only one kind of fun.

That would be too bad, because while indulging in effortless fun isn't inherently bad or "unproductive," defaulting to this choice can cut us off from a great deal of pleasure. Studies of moment-by-moment, experienced happiness find that people generally rate TV watching, for instance, as less pleasurable than reading, hobbies, and socializing. This one, simple habit change of doing a little effortful fun first can make even limited leisure time feel far more satisfying.

Participant perspectives: Getting honest about leisure time

After introducing this concept of effortful fun to Tranquility by Tuesday participants, I asked people to estimate how much time they spent on the "effortless" fun of screens. While time estimates are usually not that accurate, for the social media tallies, I suspect they were, because many people reported checking the screen-time function on their phones (thus producing specific numbers that were unlikely to be guesses). Among study participants, people averaged 48.8 minutes per weekday on social media, and 57.6 minutes per day on weekends. For TV, the estimates averaged 44.1 minutes per day on weekdays and 79.1 minutes per day on weekends. I suspect these television numbers are more likely to be underestimates, given the lack of accountability and how people tend to count TV time. (One person who claimed to watch "none" explained that "it's always kids' stuff or The Weather Channel," which isn't, in fact, none—you don't have to enjoy screen time for it to have happened!)

I also asked people to pay attention to *when* their pockets of leisure time occurred. This question produced an intriguing amount of soul-searching. It is one thing to know that you get some downtime after the kids go to bed. It is another to realize, as one person did, that you are picking up and unlocking your phone ninety-plus times per day.

Though these screen-time estimates aren't exactly huge (indeed, they are well under the population-wide average, likely because my survey participants did have such busy lives), they constitute a substantial chunk of the discretionary time that someone with a full-time job and a family could expect to log.

While a handful of people either barely touched screens at all, or felt happy with their balance, in the reflection questions, a far greater number of people noted that they weren't thrilled with their tallies, or how this time felt. One person complained that Instagram inspired her to "compare and despair." Another had this message about her screen-time number: "Please stop asking me. It's a lot, and I don't like it."

Indeed, people reported using various methods to stop the deep furrows of habit that had them swiping and tapping familiar icons. One person deleted Instagram after looking at her tallies. Another reported limiting social-media time by "Logging out of FB, uninstalling the app, and using only the browser and never ever remembering the password but rather doing 'forgot password' every time." That really raises the bar for looking at anyone's birthday-party photos.

After this accounting, I asked people what specific sort of effortful fun they thought they might like to try doing before the effortless variety. By far the most common answer was reading, though people also mentioned puzzles (including crossword puzzles or number puzzles), building LEGO sets, crafting (especially cross-stitching and knitting), playing board or card games, and actively reaching out to friends and family, whether that meant talking in person with people who lived in the same house, or calling or texting, or even writing letters.

All of these are good ideas, though reading has particular benefits to it, at least for the small chunks of time that lend themselves to app and social-media checks. If you think about it, the photo captions and comments and posts that dominate social media contain words. Looking at them is, in fact, reading. So, in many cases, choosing reading as one's effortful fun just means upgrading the reading material, rather than switching to an entirely new habit.

Why it's so hard to choose effortful fun

I asked people to plan how they might do a few minutes of effortful fun before the effortless variety, both through the day, and in the bigger chunks of leisure time that might happen at night or on weekends. What challenges might they face?

An obvious one many folks mentioned: People do not carry around books the way they carry around phones. But you can, or—more practically—you can use an e-reader app (such as Amazon's Kindle app, or Barnes & Noble's NOOK, or just use Apple's pre-installed Books app) on your phone, as Jeremy does. As a bonus, ebooks are often slightly cheaper than physical books.

Many classics are available for free or for 99 cents. The Libby app will let you borrow ebooks from your local public library. It is absolutely as easy to open the Kindle app on your phone as it is to open Facebook, Twitter, or a news app, or to wind up at those things after checking email (which is what often happens when we try to be "productive" in these little spots of time).

With a little planning, it doesn't take much effort to do effortful fun. This is true for reading in little pockets of time, and it is definitely true for the other varieties of effortful fun that people might do during longer stretches of leisure. Once the kids are in bed, there is a moment of choice. The decision to turn on the TV versus reading a book, working on a puzzle, or building a LEGO set could go either way, if the effortful fun is available.

The bigger challenge for many people turned out to be the energy required for even the smallest amount of effort:

- "Fatigue kills a lot of effortful fun."
- "My brain is pretty much mush from work the past couple days, so vegging out is easier."
- "It's so easy to turn on the TV once the kids are in bed."
- "Some nights what I thought would be fun felt like another thing I was supposed to do."

And so people found it easy to heed what one participant called "the siren song of the sofa."

Participant perspectives: Creatively overcoming challenges

I think the siren song metaphor here is apt. The sirens of Greek mythology used their overwhelmingly sweet songs to lure sailors off course. Similarly, screen-based entertainment is designed to be almost irresistibly alluring. That is the whole business model. Thousands of brilliant people have devoted their professional lives to keeping you captivated through the next commercial (or, these days, through starting the next episode in the queue), and to keep you checking back for the ninetieth time to see whether all your friends liked that post.

"It's easy to just 'check one thing' and get sucked in," one person wrote. "I have tried to do this before. Even if the book is right there and I really want to read it, if I touch the dang phone my plans go out the window."

With this reality, there are a few things you can do to lash yourself to the mast, Odysseus-style, or at least tilt the odds in effortful fun's favor.

1. Picture yourself on the other side.

Just as we learned in Chapter 6, you can picture Future You feeling satisfied at the end of a really good novel, or on the other side of any sort of effortful fun.

"I tried to remind myself that I really do love reading more than all of the effortless fun options, and although there is a sort of activation energy required to make myself open the book and settle back into the story, it's really worth it in terms of how refreshed I feel afterward," one person wrote.

Think about how it feels to have completed a thousand-piece puzzle, or to have knitted a usable hat, or to find out who did it in an Agatha Christie mystery. Then think about how you will feel after having stared at photos of gorgeous, well-coiffed families in matching outfits posing at whatever expensive vacation destination paid them to be there. This future focus isn't easy—"there needs to be a retraining of sorts in my brain," as one person put it—but it can provide a useful nudge.

2. Make effortful fun as alluring as the effortless variety.

This means taking your fun seriously. If you want to read, make sure you always have books you want to read. Splurge on that new bestseller rather than waiting for your library hold to come up. Abandon any book that is no longer compelling. You can subscribe to podcasts and newsletters with book recommendations, or work through those myriad lists of the greatest novels, or memoirs, or travel narratives.

"The nights and Sunday afternoons when I read, I had a book I really wanted to read," one participant said. "That seems to be key for me. If I'm toughing it through a book, I'm not always going to pick it up easily."

You should also fully embrace who you are as a reader. If

you hate false accusation stories, then you may as well skip any book where that's the major plot point. It's OK. There are millions of books. Even if you read a hundred books a year like Jeremy, and live for fifty more years (we can hope!) that's only five thousand more books you will read in your lifetime. You will never make it through a lot of books you'd love, so why waste time on ones you won't?

If your fun is LEGOs, then buy the sets. LEGO lovers will get more joy out of spending three weeks constructing that $200 NASA rocket than they'll get from looking at a $200 side table that just sits there. Many people pay, unthinkingly, for streaming services and cable, and then become misers with effortful fun. And maybe it does seem childish to order yet more paints or another thousand-piece puzzle, or wasteful to buy a hardcover book when your library hold will come up eventually. But then it's no wonder that effortful fun seems harder to make happen. You need to consciously work to even the game, both with resources and with the attention required to take fun seriously. Leisure time is too precious to be totally leisurely about leisure. So do what it takes to step it up—and you'll do it.

3. Set a timer.

If the previous two suggestions don't do it for you, then this one might. The rule to do effortful fun before effortless fun doesn't mean you have to do anything for hours, or that you have to forgo your effortless pleasure of choice. You can commit to doing effortful fun for just a few minutes. Ten minutes is reasonable, but even two minutes could be fine if you're reluctant. The point is to switch the automatic flow of activities. When you tell yourself that all that stands between you and a night of reading snarky replies on Twitter or binge-watching Netflix is a few minutes of effortful fun, then chances are you'll be willing to pick up your book or paintbrushes. Most likely the intrinsic fun of the activity will kick in and you'll do more. But if not, oh well. You can read a chapter in *War and Peace* in five minutes, and then spend hours watching *Selling Sunset*, and still be the kind of person who does both.

The results

Despite any concerns, the vast majority of Tranquility by Tuesday participants agreed to try this rule out. They spent the week doing a few minutes of reading, crafting, puzzles, or connecting with friends and family before turning to passive leisure. The verdict was positive: At the end of the week, the desire to continue was 6.11 on a 7-point scale, meaning almost everyone agreed or strongly agreed that this was worth trying.

And indeed, the results were impressive. By the end of the study, scores on the question of whether people felt happy with how they spent their leisure time during the previous day had risen by 20 percent. Scores on the question of whether people felt that they didn't waste time on things that were unimportant to them rose 32 percent. These numbers stayed elevated for one month and three months after the study, respectively.

This sense of not wasting time translated into all sorts of positive feelings. "Time seemed to expand," one person wrote. "It was magic." Another wrote that finally making time for effortful fun "restored my soul." Since I'm not sure anyone has ever claimed that a forty-five-minute scrolling session has restored their soul, it's not a huge leap to see that effortful fun can provide a better mental break than the effortless variety, even if it does take that slight bit of effort.

For many participants, this sense of time expanding happened because doing effortful fun made their limited leisure time feel more memorable. As they were actively choosing to do something satisfying with their leisure time amid the daily chaos, they became more aware that this leisure time was happening. The time was spent mindfully, rather than mindlessly. This meant that even limited leisure time felt more robust than it might have in comparison with other activities.

"This week was very busy work-wise, and without this effortful fun it would most likely have felt even worse and even more overwhelming," one person wrote. "Then I would have felt as if I had done nothing but work. With the effortful fun, the workweek felt at least a little bit better and as if I at least had some time for myself." When you look back over a whirlwind week and see that you still managed to read an entire novel—doable for many books in about thirty minutes a day—this can change the entire narrative. Life isn't all a slog. Amid the chaos there is still time for whatever you happen to enjoy.

As people began to use their time confetti for effortful fun, some were inspired to look for more of it. "It's almost like a treasure hunt in my days," one person wrote. "Where/what can I fit in to make me feel happier and more productive?"

This sense of being happier came up a lot in the answers. "I feel more optimistic and energetic," one person wrote. Others noted a general feeling of tranquility that led to increased patience and engagement, both at home and at work.

I suspect that this happiness is at least partly due to a sense of making progress, which some research has found is key to workplace satisfaction, and probably matters for our personal lives too. Effortless fun often lacks this element of progress. Not always—watching a full scripted series to completion can be satisfying—but often. You will never reach the end of Instagram. You *will* see results when you do twelve of the two hundred and fifty steps in that LEGO set. Your bookmark will move forward when you read another seventy-five pages. "I finished a book in under three days and it was awesome," one person wrote. Another noted that "I never would have found the time to make progress on this [creative] project if I hadn't been following this rule! This is a game changer for me."

When we actively choose how to spend our time, we become more satisfied with it. "I was happy that I got this reading done and was not half-watching the same reruns of a TV show before going to bed," one person wrote. "It felt like I was actually using my time wisely—taking control of that time rather than doing something mindless."

In many cases, screen-based fun is a reactive decision. It is automatic, and losing hours to it unintentionally can make us feel reactive about time in general. We can feel depleted, and like time is happening to us without our permission. Making mindful decisions, on the other hand, is energizing. Someone who reflected on the rule noted that "Comparing the evenings I spent scrolling to the evenings I spent reading this week, I can say that I get a lot more out of reading. Random scrolling just swallows time and suddenly you realize that you have done this for thirty minutes."

This general boost in energy played out in all sorts of unexpected ways. One Tranquility by Tuesday respondent reported that committing to do effortful fun before effortless fun finally "made sex happen!" No, sex was not the effortful fun in question (though it could be!). Instead, this couple realized that "If we watch TV right after dinner and wait until we're in bed to see if we're both 'in the mood,' we're usually too tired to make it happen." But when they both read instead, they still had enough energy to enjoy all sorts of fun—a magical outcome indeed.

Daydreaming counts

Only a few folks felt this rule was not for them—but after reading their explanations, in many cases, I felt like we were still getting at the same thing.

For instance, one person wrote of disagreeing that leisure time needed to be effortful.

"I'll often just relax on the bed with the baby, and just do nothing," this person wrote, with "nothing" defined as, in essence, daydreaming. "I do strongly agree that just finding an activity that doesn't really fill you up, like useless phone scrolling, should be avoided. But if I'm already not doing those activities (phone scrolling, TV time) I'm also happy to just relax and do nothing, say for thirty minutes a day, instead of having all leisure activity be effortful. This 'relax/do nothing' was actually something I consciously learned during the pandemic, to proactively slow down and find 'me time.'"

I'm quite OK with this. Indeed, I'd say that consciously choosing to do "nothing" in a world with constant digital access does require a fair amount of effort. While I want people to read or make space for other such kinds of fun, the bigger point of this rule is to crowd out the mindless activities that tend to consume a bigger portion of the day than people would like—the useless phone scrolling that this new parent was choosing not to do. So yes, admire a sleeping baby. Go somewhere beautiful, or sit by a big window in bad weather, and just take the world in. Have your morning cup of coffee outside and don't look at your phone until you've reached the bottom of your mug. I wouldn't call this doing "nothing." It is finding time for wonder—time that in our distracted world is often in short supply.

Changing our relationship with leisure

A more common lament with doing effortful fun first was that people grew frustrated with fitting their fun into short periods of time. A good-enough book will have you hoping that colleagues will dial in late to calls. You are probably best off accepting that, as one person put it, "shorter amounts of fun are better than none."

However, you can also channel this frustration toward finding longer blocks of time for effortful fun. The time is often there, even in busy lives—a more nuanced point that often surfaced during the COVID-19 pandemic and the discussion of how people spend their downtime.

In the early days of lockdown, people turned to many effortful fun activities for the first time in a while. Headlines blared that we had forever changed our over-scheduled ways. We would embrace a slower pace of life! It is true that there was a run on commercially packaged yeast thanks to all the new bakers. A LEGO set I had my eye on sold out quickly (I had to resort to eBay). The general feeling, as Riche Holmes Grant, an entrepreneur, content creator, and mother, put it to me, was "when else would I have this opportunity when the world slows down to do things like [virtual] floral design classes?"

Riche was as immersed in the world's prior swiftness as everyone else—a swiftness that seemed to preclude many forms of effortful fun. She had worked one summer in law school at the

Guggenheim museum in New York City, and had bought a LEGO set depicting the museum to commemorate the experience. The set then proceeded to sit there on her shelf, untouched, for years as she spent her time traveling to meetings and shuttling her daughter Riley to ballet and a host of other activities.

Then the pandemic cleared the schedule. With little else competing for time, Riche pulled the Guggenheim set off her shelf. She built it. She began buying more LEGO sets. She built the set depicting major Paris landmarks. She built a LEGO floral array. Her appetite for effortful fun whetted, she began trying floral design and painting too, among other hobbies.

The pandemic opened her eyes to the possibility of making time for creative pursuits outside her paid work—and yet, she acknowledges that she could have found an hour here and there in the past too. Even the most complicated LEGO set might take a dozen hours or so. There are 8,760 hours in a year. Whatever else someone has going on in life, a LEGO set doesn't actually have to sit untouched for decades.

Instead, what happens is more a phenomenon of near infinite choice. One fascinating study found that higher-income people felt more time stress than lower-income people, even when they were spending the same amount of time in paid or household work. The higher-income people's money enabled more choices for what they could do with their leisure time, but they still had twenty-four hours in a day, like everyone else.

Hence, the time stress. Basically, when everything under the sun is an option, then we feel like we have less time, because the plethora of options makes us feel like we might be making the wrong choice.

"That's how the world works," Riche says. "When you don't do it, you wonder, am I missing out? Are my kids missing out?"

In that wariness, in that desire to leave options open, we have a tendency to choose things that don't feel so much like choices. When we are on social media, we could in an instant switch over to being productive in our inboxes, whereas constructing the Guggenheim out of LEGOs is a flag on the hill that, yep, I am claiming this time for leisure. During the pandemic, when you couldn't go to ballet, or with colleagues to a restaurant, or to a nonprofit board meeting, time seemed less fraught, and so people looked for ways to actively fill it, rather than passively spend it.

What changed for Riche is not how much time she has, but rather, the realization that effortful leisure is a wonderful thing, and should be a priority among competing activities. These days, even as the world opens up, when she has some downtime, Riche still chooses to paint rather than catch up on a show.

When we put effortful fun first, we do not mindlessly watch our lives get eaten away with time that makes us feel less rejuvenated than when we started. Nothing needs to disappear from life, but the balance changes.

"I am still doing the effortless things, but now in the evenings I try to prioritize the effortful and as a result have flipped the amount of time I spend on each type of activity," one Tranquility by Tuesday participant wrote, three months after the project ended. "Instead of twenty minutes scrolling and five minutes reading before bed, it's now twenty minutes reading and five minutes scrolling most nights."

In an incredibly busy life, this person has now found almost two more hours each week to read. She is wasting less time on what doesn't matter. That is the power of this simple rule.

Take the next step

◆ ──────────

UPGRADE YOUR BITS OF TIME

Reading remains the easiest form of effortful fun for small blocks of time. If you feel like these little bits of time are slipping away from you, then start reinforcing the habit of "effortful before effortless" by reading before scrolling.

But once you've become comfortable with that, you might branch out in these small moments, which turn out to be quite numerous once you start noticing them. Lots of hobbies—even unexpected ones—might lend themselves to becoming micro-hobbies, with progress possible in minutes. For example:

MUSIC: If you play the piano (or, perhaps, an electronic keyboard with headphones after your kids go to bed), or any other sort of instrument, you could use bits of time through the day to watch YouTube videos of other musicians performing the piece you are learning. By the time you sit down to practice at night, you will have absorbed these multiple interpretations, and have new insights into how you might play the piece. If you work at home, keep your instrument nearby. You might be able to practice a tricky section a few times if a call gets canceled, and maybe a few more times later while you're preheating the oven for dinner.

ART: Most people won't tote their oil paints and easels to their workplaces. But if, for instance, you are painting a garden scene of hummingbirds, you could order a beautiful book of hummingbird illustrations and page through that between meetings or appointments with patients. You can also look at many museums' collections online for inspiration. In five minutes you could compare how three different artists depicted apples, giving you ideas for your own weekend still-life painting session. You might even start sketching a preparatory study in a longer gap. And other sorts of art lend themselves even better to time confetti. Snap a dozen photos of an intriguing shadow you spot on a walk. You can pick up and put down a cross-stitched scene without much bother, or use a digital scrapbooking app.

BAKING: An aspiring baker might use bits of time to peruse new recipes or watch videos of a technique that's tricky to master. Creating a social-media account that follows only bakeries and food stylists could keep these bits of time focused on creativity; reading food blogs will likewise feel more rejuvenating than refreshing headlines.

GARDENING: Skim lists of ornamental trees you might purchase for your garden, and study layouts of fine landscaping in other places. Read an article in a gardening magazine or flip through books from the library on gardens in a completely different climate. On work-from-home days, wear pants that can get a little dirty. Ten minutes is plenty of time to yank a few weeds, plant a few bulbs, or trim some stems to put in a vase on your desk.

It might help to think of your favorite effortful fun as a quest. How can you find a handful of moments through the day to advance in this adventure? This nudges the mindset toward curiosity, rather than forced productivity. No one needs to use every minute. But on the other hand, I believe that even mere minutes are worthy enough not to be wasted. Anything we want to do in life takes time. Being willing to use the little bits opens up possibility—and far more joy than we might have imagined.

Your turn

---◆---

EFFORTFUL BEFORE EFFORTLESS

Planning questions:

1. What are your favorite sorts of effortful fun—that is, fun that requires some planning, coordination, or mindfulness?

2. What leisure activities do you typically do at night in the hours before bed or during downtime on weekends?

3. How much time, in minutes, do you estimate you spend on social media on a typical weekday? What about on weekends? When do these minutes happen?

4. How much time, in minutes, do you estimate you spend on TV or other video entertainment on a typical weekday? How about on weekends?

5. Today, choose one form of "effortful" fun to do before screen time. What will this be?

6. What challenges might you encounter in doing effortful fun before effortless fun?

7. What needs to happen to ensure you spend time on this effortful fun activity first?

Implementation questions:

1. Think back over the past week. What sorts of "effortful" fun did you make time for?

2. When did you choose to make time for this effortful fun?

3. What effects did you see in your life from making time for effortful fun?

4. What challenges did you face while trying to do effortful fun before effortless fun?

5. How did you address these challenges?

6. If you modified this rule, how did you do so?

7. How likely are you to continue using this rule in your life?

CONCLUSION

*A*ny good performer knows this formula for astonishing an audience: You boost the difficulty level by degrees, until no one can believe what you're doing. The acrobat balances on a sphere, which seems wobbly enough. So naturally he adds a plate atop his head, and then a stack of dishes, one at a time, halfway to the ceiling. First the clown juggles four balls. Then five. Two more get thrown into the mix. Once it seems like he just couldn't add more, the lights go out. The balls light up. He's juggling in the dark!

I find such performances mesmerizing. Perhaps it's because life often feels like a similar circus act. You rate weeks by degree of difficulty. This one starts with a business trip and a contractor needing to come repair the roof. Not too bad. Then we add a back-up childcare arrangement and the dog eating something that disagrees with him. The audience is starting to murmur. We throw in a new client's request for a proposal, a fender bender in a parking lot, and a child's discovery that his dress pants don't fit on the morning of a major performance. Another child announces that he has just joined an after-school club that meets on varying days for varying amounts of time. That's why he didn't take the bus home this afternoon and is texting you that someone needs to come pick him up in the next ten minutes. The audience leans forward. Which balls are about to go flying?

The project of constructing a good life can be complicated. This is particularly true when it involves building a demanding career, raising a family, or throwing yourself into any other meaningful pursuit. And yet, if you study any good circus performer, you can see that what looks chaotic often isn't at all. All is well rehearsed. Adjustments are made as needed. There are good systems for managing the rising levels of difficulty. Look closely and the face under that wobbling stack of china can be serene. This is just another day on the job. Amid the ridiculousness, it is even possible to have fun.

This is how I think of the Tranquility by Tuesday rules. These habits take effort to build into our lives. But once they become part of the background narrative, they can calm the chaos and help us make time for what matters—even as life's circus continues. It is folly to hope the circus will slow down anytime soon. These habits can help us enjoy life as it is now. What seems hard at first can, over time, start to feel easy.

To see if that was the case, I followed up with Tranquility by

Tuesday participants in August 2021, six months after the project began and three months after it ended. I asked people for their reflections, both on the project and how it had shaped their lives.

The good news is that time satisfaction scores remained elevated. Scores across my time-satisfaction scale for how people spent their time *yesterday*, which incorporated questions about energy, progress on goals, and not wasting time, rose 15 percent from the initial survey to the final follow-up. Scores on how satisfied people were with how they spent their time *generally* were up 18 percent. These are all statistically significant results.

I asked people to reflect on the specific changes they had made. While people cited practical benefits of individual rules, when they thought about all these rules together, many noted that the biggest change had been in how they perceived time and their lives.

"Overall, it's led to a more intentional effort in how I spend my time—primarily in getting past the sense that my life was an unending to-do list," one person wrote.

Another who spoke of intentionality noted that "I'm most proud of changing the story that I tell myself. I do have time for the things that are important to me and time for fun too."

For many people, adopting a weekly perspective was particularly helpful in shifting from a perception of time scarcity to time abundance.

"I absolutely look at time by the week now, and it's opened up so much in my planning abilities," one participant wrote. "I feel like I have a better sense of being able to prioritize things I want to accomplish [and] I don't feel like I'm failing when I don't make daily progress. Weekly progress matters!" Another wrote that "instead of focusing on a 'lost' day, I look at the broader picture (in planning and in retrospect)."

Often, the rules themselves had become mantras. "Some parts of Tranquility by Tuesday have become inner dialogue," one person said. "For example, after the kids go to bed, I think about what I want to do, and I hear 'effortful before effortless!' Sometimes I go with it, sometimes I don't, but I follow it way more than I used to!"

As these rules echoed in people's heads—I like to think they're hearing my voice—they began enjoying more tranquility in their lives. "Because I am naturally high-strung, I get anxious about time and getting enough done," one person wrote. "Through the Tranquility by Tuesday project I am realizing [life] is more than putting my head down and working." With the mantra to plan in "one big adventure, one little adventure," this person reported making space for little adventures during the week, like attending a Zoom session presented by the local art museum. As life featured more than to-dos to be anxious about, time itself began to be transformed.

There was more fun, and more sense of calm amid the bustle.

"I think the thing I am most proud of is feeling more in control," one person wrote, citing the example of "doing things like taking time for professional development at work earlier in the week rather than leaving it to Fridays, and then using Fridays for back-up slots and planning. This has enabled me to feel that I am less led by work crises and more adaptable as well as being able to cope with what comes up in the week."

Time is both precious and plentiful, and as people changed their perception of hours, they began leaning into this paradox.

"I think I'm getting more protective of my time, saying no not only to more things that don't feel connected to my top priorities, but also putting myself more wholeheartedly into the things that are the best uses of my time," one person wrote. "I'm taking better care of myself and my most meaningful relationships. Honestly, I'm proud of myself for participating in this study during an incredibly challenging time of my life."

It was, indeed, a challenging time. It continues to be a challenging time as I write this in early 2022, with new pandemic variants again wreaking havoc on schedules. Who knows what crises will be next? None of us can fully shape the forces that in turn shape our lives. And yet despite that larger swirling, there is still much of time we can direct, and even with the things we can't direct, we can direct how we feel.

"At a time of absolute chaos, this project made me feel optimistic," one person wrote. "I needed that. Very much."

I need it too. And so, moving through the daily circus of my life, I do my best to live by these rules. I go to bed on time, plan my weeks on Fridays, get up to move by midday, make sure that anything I care about—such as family meals—happens at least three times a week, build in open space and back-up slots, plan my adventures, take my night off for choir practice, batch my small tasks, and read or do my puzzles before scrolling through headlines. Well, I do these things some of the time. Some days the rules feel more achievable than others. But I do know it is during the frenzied times, when the three-ring circus is going at full tilt, when I am surrounded by boxes after moving, school has gone virtual, my new refrigerator has disappeared into supply-chain limbo, and I'm facing down multiple deadlines, that these rules matter the most.

"I think this project has been very helpful in establishing habits and helping me avoid the myth that I don't have time to do the things I want to do," one person wrote. "I definitely have the time, I just have to exercise the discipline."

So do we all. The good news is that everything becomes easier over time, as the grooves of habit wear deep. So why not start now? I am not promising that the Tranquility by Tuesday rules will work miracles overnight. Some rules take time to take effect. But I do know from thousands of data points and a novel's worth of time observations that these rules are proven winners. If other busy people like you found them useful, most likely you will too. Some rules will change your life by this Tuesday. And others? Their magic will slowly make life feel more doable, for all the Tuesdays to come.

ACKNOWLEDGMENTS

I am grateful to everyone who helped with the Tranquility by Tuesday project, and with this book.

First, I appreciate that so many people took the time to participate in the survey, both in a pilot phase in the fall of 2020, and then for the main phase in the spring of 2021. People shared their challenges and triumphs, and their insightful answers made this book possible. I'm also grateful to the people who agreed to "time makeovers" for my blog as I was narrowing down the Tranquility by Tuesday rules. Many of those stories made it into the book, as well as insights from experts and other fascinating people.

I'm grateful to Jessica Webb for designing the Tranquility by Tuesday survey, and compiling and analyzing the results. Her attention to detail, and eye for answers worth highlighting, made writing this book a far more tranquil experience than it could have been.

In order to recruit people for the Tranquility by Tuesday project, and to design and manage the emails to participants, I needed a good digital team. Fortunately, Nancy Sheed and Lizzy Fox made sure that thousands of nice-looking messages went to the right places.

I'm grateful to Emilie Stewart for helping shape the proposal and for working with Portfolio to figure out the book's contours. Many thanks to Leah Trouwborst for acquiring the book, and to Kimberly Meilun for her thoughtful and patient edits, and to the rest of the team at Portfolio for copyediting, design, and publicity.

Over the years, I've talked about many of the ideas in this book on my podcasts. I'm grateful to Sarah Hart-Unger for being an enthusiastic cohost for "Best of Both Worlds," and to iHeart-Media (and particularly Lowell Brillante) for producing the "Before Breakfast" podcast.

Writing can sometimes be a solitary endeavor, so I appreciate the support of other writers. Katherine Lewis and KJ Dell'Antonia have provided weekly accountability support, and my writing strategy group of Chris Bailey, Camille Pagán, Katherine J. Chen, and Anne Bogel has given me lots of great ideas (and steered me away from my bad ones). I'm also grateful to some other writing and accountability groups that I am part of, but that operate anonymously. Secrets can keep life interesting.

And speaking of keeping life interesting, my family keeps giving me new material to write about. Many thanks to Michael for his support, and the kids—Jasper, Sam, Ruth, Alex, and Henry—for going along with my ideas for adventures. Life is often a circus, but I think we do a pretty good job achieving Tranquility by Tuesday—and having a lot of fun along the way.

APPENDIX

The Time-Satisfaction Scale

Please indicate how much you agree with each of the following statements (strongly disagree to strongly agree).

> (1 = strongly disagree; 2 = disagree; 3 = disagree somewhat; 4 = neither agree nor disagree; 5 = agree somewhat; 6 = agree; 7 = strongly agree)

Yesterday, I had enough time for the things I wanted to do.

1   2   3   4   5   6   7

Yesterday, I got enough sleep to feel well rested.

1   2   3   4   5   6   7

Yesterday, I made progress on my professional goals.

1   2   3   4   5   6   7

Yesterday, I made progress on my personal goals.

1   2   3   4   5   6   7

Yesterday, I had enough energy to handle my responsibilities.

1   2   3   4   5   6   7

Yesterday, I was happy with how I spent my leisure time.

1   2   3   4   5   6   7

Yesterday, I did not waste time on things that weren't important to me.

1   2   3   4   5   6   7

Generally, I have enough time for the things I want to do.

1   2   3   4   5   6   7

Generally, I have the energy for the things I want to do.

1   2   3   4   5   6   7

Overall, I feel good about my relationships and
my progress on my personal priorities.

1   2   3   4   5   6   7

Overall, I'm making progress on my professional goals.

1   2   3   4   5   6   7

Generally, how I spend my time aligns with my
priorities and values.

1   2   3   4   5   6   7

I regularly have time just for me.

1   2   3   4   5   6   7

NOTES

5 **in 2020, the average person slept:** American Time Use Survey, Table 1, "Time spent in primary activities and percent of the population engaging in each activity, averages for May to December, 2019 and 2020," www.bls .gov/news.release/atus.t01.htm.

5 **employed parents with kids:** American Time Use Survey, Table 8B, "Time spent in primary activities for the civilian population 18 years and over by presence and age of youngest household child and sex, 2019 annual averages, employed," U.S. Bureau of Labor Statistics, www.bls.gov/news .release/atus.t08b.htm.

6 **sociologist Arlie Hochschild once wrote:** Arlie Hochschild, *The Second Shift: Working Families and the Revolution at Home* (New York: Penguin, 1989), 10.

7 **annual Sleep in America poll:** National Sleep Foundation, Sleep in America Poll 2020 press release: "Americans Feel Sleepy 3 Days a Week,

With Impacts on Activities, Mood & Acuity," www.thensf.org/wp-content/uploads/2020/03/SIA-2020-Report.pdf.

23 **according to Spall:** Benjamin Spall, interview with the author.

45 **famous quote from Dwight Eisenhower:** Dwight Eisenhower, "Remarks at the National Defense Executive Reserve Conference," November 14, 1957, www.presidency.ucsb.edu/documents/remarks-the-national-defense-executive-reserve-conference.

59 **Regular exercise turns out:** For instance, see S. Kvam, C. L. Kleppe, I. H. Nordhus, and A. Hovland, "Exercise as a treatment for depression: a meta-analysis," *J. Affect Disord* 202 (2016): 67–86.

59 **Exercise works as well as:** For instance, see Giselle Soares Passos et al., "Is exercise an alternative treatment for chronic insomnia?" *Clinics* (Sao Paulo, Brazil) 67, no. 6 (2012): 653–60. https://doi:10.6061/clinics/2012(06)17.

59 **One study found:** Polaski, Phelps, Szucs, Ramsey, Kostek, and Kolber, "The dosing of aerobic exercise therapy on experimentally-induced pain in healthy female participants," *Scientific Reports* 9, no. 1 (2019): 14842. https://doi:10.1038/s41598-019-51247-0.

60 **studies of people's energy levels:** Janeta Nikolovski and Jack Groppel, "The power of an energy microburst," white paper (2013), www.researchgate.net/publication/280683168_The_power_of_an_energy_microburst.

124 **I came across one:** Sendhil Mullainathan and Eldar Shafir, *Scarcity: Why Having Too Little Means So Much* (New York: Times Books, 2013), 183–86.

193 **from appointment to appointment:** Leo Tolstoy, *War and Peace*, trans. Ann Dunnigan (New York: Signet Classic, 1968), 522.

218 **Among U.S. social-media users:** Statista Research Department, "Average daily time spent on social media by U.S. adults 2017–2022," April 28, 2021, www.statista.com/statistics/324267/us-adults-daily-facebook-minutes.

218 **the average person with a full-time job:** American Time Use Survey, Table 9, "Time spent in leisure and sports activities by selected

characteristics, averages for May to December, 2019 and 2020," www.bls
.gov/news.release/atus.t09.htm.

233 **One fascinating study found:** Daniel S. Hamermesh and Jungmin Lee,
"Stressed Out on Four Continents: Time Crunch or Yuppie Kvetch?"
National Bureau of Economic Research Working Paper Series, no. 10186
(December 2003), www.nber.org/papers/w10186.